The Beloved

The Beloved

*Reflections on the
Path of the Heart*

BY

KAHLIL GIBRAN

TRANSLATED BY JOHN WALBRIDGE

WHITE CLOUD PRESS
ASHLAND, OREGON

99 98 97   5 4 3 2

Cover Illustration by Kahlil Gibran, "The Flame," Courtesy of Harvard
University Art Museums, Gift of Mrs. Reginald A. Daly
Cover Design by Daniel Cook
Printed in the United States of America

Library of Congress Cataloging in Publication Data

Gibran, Kahlil, 1883-1931
    [Selections. English. 1994]]
    The beloved: reflections on the path of the heart / Kahlil Gibran;
translated by John Walbridge. -- 1st ed..
        p.   cm.
    ISBN 1-883991-05-6 " $17.00
    I. Walbridge, John.   II. Title.
PJ7826.I2A77 1994 1994
892'.78503--dc20   94-19371
                                                CIP

Illustration credits
All illustrations by Kahlil Gibran
Nude with dancers, p.9; Mother and Child, p. 22; The Summit, p. 55;
Man and Woman Kissing, p. 91; Self-portrait, back cover, Gifts of Mrs.
Mary Haskell Minis, in the collection of the Telfair Academy of Arts and
Sciences, Savannah, Georgia. The Flame, p. 109, Courtesy of Harvard
University Art Museums, Gift of Mrs. Reginald A. Daly.

Note on texts

The pieces translated in this volume are taken from Michail Naimy, ed., *al-Majmuʿah al-kámila li-muʾallifát Jibrán Khalíl Jibrán,* Beirut, 1961, and were originally published in various Arabic papers and journals. They are "Alá Báb al-Haykal," pp. 370–372; "Aghniyat al-Layl," p. 595; "Agháni," pp. 328–331; "Warda al-Hání," pp. 81–95; "al-Jiníya al-sáhira," pp. 376–377; "Hayát al-Hubb," pp. 236–237; "Hikáya," pp. 238–240; "al-Rafíqa," pp. 287–288; "Malikat al-Khiyál," pp. 281–282; "al-Sulm," pp. 306–307; "Hadíth al-hubb," pp. 302-304; "Munáját," pp. 284–285; "Qabl al-intihár," pp. 378–379; "Bayn al-Kharáʾib," pp. 253–254; "Ibtisáma wa-Damʿa," pp. 247–249; "Munáját arwáh," pp. 316–319; "Madjaʿ al-ʿArús," pp. 106-115; "Biʾlláh yá Qalbí," p. 592; "Makhbʾát al-Sudúr," pp. 293-295; "Banaát al-Bahr," pp. 245-246; "Bil-Ams waʾl-Yawm wa-Ghadan," p. 218; "Ayyuháʾl-Layl," pp. 373-375.

To the spirit that embraced my spirit, to the heart that poured its secrets into my heart, to the hand that kindled the fire of my emotions, I dedicate this book.

GIBRAN

This was Gibran's dedication of his collection Rebellious Spirits, *in which the stories "Rose al-Hani" and "The Bridal Bed" appeared. It is addressed to his friend and patron Mary Haskell.*

Translator's dedication:
To Linda, from whom I came to understand such things

CONTENTS

INTRODUCTION

*K*ahlil Gibran was born in 1883 in Bisharri, a Maronite Christian village in the mountains of northern Lebanon. His mother was from a family of priests; his father was a minor agent of the local warlord. His childhood was spent in desperate poverty in this place of great beauty. A family friend taught the young Kahlil how to read. When he was 12, his mother attempted to escape her troubles by emigrating to the United States with her children. From the ethereal beauty of the Lebanese mountains, Kahlil found himself amidst the squalor of the Boston slums. His mother scraped out a meager living for herself and her children as a peddler.

The young Kahlil's lovely drawings attracted the attention of a social worker, who put him in touch with Fred Holland Day, an avant-garde photographer and publisher, who used Gibran and his family as models and introduced Gibran to the literary world of 1890s Boston. His new friends, charmed by this talented Lebanese boy, introduced him to modern art, gave him books to read by such authors as Nietzsche, and took him to plays and concerts. Thus, although his education in America was very uneven—he never really learned to spell, for example, and was always more comfortable writing in Arabic—he became accustomed to traveling in literary circles while still a teenager living with his family amidst the poverty of the Syrian ghetto in Boston's South End.

In 1896, he returned to Lebanon for high school, where he acquired the rudiments of an Arabic literary education. He returned to America and his intellectual friends in 1902. Soon after his mother, sister, and half-brother died, leaving him alone in America with his surviving sister. During the next few years he began working seriously as an artist and attracted somewhat wider attention, even exhibiting in a small way. He also began to write for the Arabic newspapers published in America. His prose poems, simple parables written without the rhetorical elaborations of traditional Arabic poetry, quickly made him a major figure among Arabic writers in America. In 1908 one of his American friends, Mary Haskell, supplied the funds for him to go to Paris to study art.

Returning to America in 1910, he worked continuously on his drawings and paintings and continued to write for the Arabic newspapers. In 1912 he moved to New York to be closer to the centers of art and Arabic literature in America. His art earned him only a precarious living, and he was forced to depend on the assistance of friends, particularly Mary Haskell, a talented and independent woman who was the headmistress of a girls' school in Boston. When Gibran began writing seriously in English, she served as his editor; the form of his English writings owes much to her assistance and judgment. His first English work was *The Wanderer,* a collection of prose poems and parables. By this time he was well established as a major modern Arabic writer. *The Prophet,* his best known work, was written over a number of years and finally published in 1923. This and the other English works that followed it eventually gave Gibran a degree of financial independence. He continued to work on his paintings, but his health began to deteriorate. He died on April 10, 1931. Despite the objections of the church authorities, who had been offended by his anti-clerical writings, he received a religious funeral. At his instructions, his body was taken back to be buried in his home village of Bisharri and the royalties of his books were divided between his sister, the only surviving member of his immediate family, and his village.

Gibran is first of all an Arabic writer. Arabic was his native language and the language he was always most comfortable with. Even after living in America for most of his life, he would still write a poem first in Arabic and then translate it into English. His Arabic works are remarkable, free of the exaggerated rhetoric and strict traditional forms characteristic of Arabic poetry up to his time. His simple diction and new forms revolutionized Arabic literature. Except for a short novel, *Broken Wings,* a verse dialogue, *Processions,* and some one-act plays, all of his Arabic writings were in the form of short pieces—

stories, parables, and prose poems—written for newspapers and magazines. Many were later collected and published as books.

The themes of his Arabic works are familiar to readers of his English works: nature against society, spirituality, natural beauty, human injustice, and the destruction of the spirit by society. Most of his Arabic works were written before his books in English. They are more passionate and fresh, on the whole, than the English work, being products of his youth. The influences that shaped his writing were obvious. Most important was the contrast between the beauty of his native Lebanese mountains and the squalor of Boston and New York, where he lived most of his life. Lebanon, romanticized by exile, is the real setting of all his works. He championed the freedom and simplicity of the individual against the rigidities of society and protested the oppression of the weak, the poor, and women. He denounced the hypocrisy of organized religion, particularly his own Maronite church. Though his romanticism and anarchism may seem naive, the intensity of his feelings, the energy of his ideas, and the universality of the disquiet which he voices speak to modern men and women.

Gibran's Arabic writings were translated after his death. These translations are not particularly good. Most are more or less inelegant and some are extremely inaccurate and misleading. Gibran's reputation has suffered from them. We undertook the present series to provide fresh, contemporary, and accurate translations of Gibran's significant Arabic work. The translations follow the original as closely as practical without doing violence to English style. We have not tried to imitate Gibran's English style since we think that his Arabic works deserve to be judged on their own considerable merits.

The pieces in this volume each deal with romantic love. Romantic love, like life, was an absolute ideal for Gibran. Many of these pieces tell of the bitter unhappiness caused by the subordination of romantic love and personal happiness to worldly calculation. He saw women as the particular victims of rigid social customs and expectations and of standards that made marriage an economic transaction. The love of a man and a woman was a pure emotion, more spiritual than sexual, and was not to be compromised.

Gibran was deeply fond of women, understood them, and sympathized with their plight. He himself never married, so his ideal of love always remained the ethereal delights of courtship rather than the calmer happiness of stable marriage. His life was marked by a series of profound friendships with women: his mother and his two sisters, to whom he was devoted; Josephine Peabody, the Cambridge society intellectual who befriended him as a teenager; Hala al-Daher, the woman in Lebanon who was his first love; Micheline, a beautiful French artist; May Ziadeh, the Arab writer whom he never met in person; Barbara Young, his supporter in his last years; and, most important, Mary Haskell, who was his friend, patron, and editor for half his life. The most important of these friendships were platonic, marked by deep and thoughtful friendship. These relationships shaped his art, his writing, and his life.[†]

In the absence of a critical edition, we have followed the text of the collected edition of his Arabic works published by his friend Mikhail Naimy.

John Walbridge

[†] The story of these relationships is told in fascinating detail in *Kahlil Gibran: His Life and World* by Jean and Kahlil Gibran, Boston, New York Graphic Society, 1974. A selection of his correspondence with Mary Haskell is in *Beloved Prophet: The Love Letters of Kahlil Gibran and Mary Haskell and Her Private Journal*, New York, Alfred A. Knopf, 1972.

At the Gate of the Temple

I purified my lips with sacred fire that I might speak of love, but when I opened my mouth to speak, I found myself mute.

I sang the melodies of a love I did not yet know, but when I came to know it, the words became a muffled whisper in my mouth, the songs in my breast a profound silence.

In the past, O people, you asked me about the wonders and delights of love, and you found satisfaction in what I told you. But now, when love has draped me with its robes, I in my turn come to ask you about its ways and virtues. Is there one among you who can answer me? I come to ask you about what is in me and wish you to tell me of my own soul. Is there one among you who can explain my heart to my own heart, who can explain my essence to my essence itself?

Will you not tell me what is this fire kindled in my breast? It consumes my faculties and melts my emotions and desires.

What are these invisible hands, soft yet coarse, that grip my spirit in my hours of solitude and loneliness? Into my heart they pour wine mixed with the bitterness of pleasure and the sweetness of pain.

What are these wings rustling about my couch in the silence of the night as I watch wakeful for what I know not, listening to what I do not hear, staring at what I do not see, pondering what I do not comprehend, aware of what I do not apprehend, sighing because in sighs are the groanings more beloved to me than the echoes of laughter and joy, submitting to an unseen power that slays me, then give me life, then slays me again and again until dawn breaks and light fills the corners of my room. Then I sleep. Yet behind my spent eyelids forms of wakefulness dance and on my stoney blanket sway the phantoms of dreams.

What is this which we call "love"?

Tell me what is this hidden mystery concealed beyond the ages, lurking behind appearances, yet making its home in the heart of being?

What is this unconditioned thought that comes as the cause of all effects, as the effect of all causes?

What is this wakefulness that encompasses both death and life and molds them into a dream stranger than life and deeper than death?

Tell me, O people, tell me! Who among you would not wake from the sleep of life if love were to brush your spirit with its fingertips?

Who among you would not forsake your father and your mother and your home if the girl whom your heart loved were to call to him?

Who among you would not cross the seas, traverse deserts, go over mountains and valleys to reach the woman whom his spirit has chosen?

What youth would not follow his heart to the ends of the earth to breath the sweetness of his lover's breath, feel the soft touch of her hands, delight in the melody of her voice?

What man would not immolate his soul that its smoke might rise to a god who would hear his plea and answer his prayer?

Yesterday I stood by the gate of the temple and asked passersby about the mysteries and virtues of love.

A man of middle years passed by, his body wasted, his face dark. Sighing, he said, "Love has made weak the strength I inherited from the First Man."

A youth, his body strong and brawny, passed by. In a voice of song he said, "Love is resolution added to my being, linking my present to generations past and future."

A woman, her eyes melancholy, passed by and, sighing, said, "Love is a deadly poison, the breath of black adders writhing in Hell, flowing and swirling through the sky until it falls covered in dew, only to be lapped up by thirsty spirits. Then they are drunk for a moment, sober for a year, dead for eternity."

A rosy cheeked girl passed by and said, smiling, "Love is a fountain whose waters the spirit brides pour into the spirits of the strong, making them to ascend in prayer among the stars of night and to sing songs of praise before the sun by day."

A man passed by. His clothes were black, his beard long. Frowning, he said, "Love is blind ignorance. It begins at youth's beginning and ends with its end."

A handsome man with open features passed and gaily said, "Love is celestial knowledge that lights our eyes and shows us things as the gods see them."

A blind man passed, tapping the earth with his cane, and weeping, he said, "Love is a thick mist enshrouding the soul on all sides and veiling the outlines of existence from it—or allowing it to see only the spectres of its desires wandering among the rocks, deaf to the sounds of its own cries echoing in the valley."

A youth carrying a guitar passed and sang out, "Love is a magical ray of light shining out from the depths of the sensitive being and illuminating all around it. You see the world as a procession traveling through green meadows, life as a lovely dream erected between wakefulness and wakefulness."

An old man passed. His back was bent, his feet dragged like pieces of cloth. In a quavering voice he said, "Love is rest for the body in the silence of the tomb, peace for the soul in the depths of eternity."

A child of five years passed and laughed back to me, "Love is my father, love is my mother. Only my father and my mother know love."

The day went by. The people passed before the temple, each describing himself as he spoke of love, revealing his hopes and telling of the mystery of life.

When evening came and the movement of passersby was stilled, I heard a voice from within the temple: "Life has two halves: one patient and one afire. Love is the fiery half."

At that I entered the temple and bowed down in earnest, silent prayer, "Make me, O Lord, food for the flames. Consume me, O God, in the sacred fire. Amen."

NIGHT SONGS

Silent is the night, but in the robe of silence
dreams lie waiting.
The moon rolls overhead.
Its watchful eyes observe
the passing days.

Let me take you,
daughter of the fields, to the
lovers' vineyard.
The wine we press will quench the
fires of longing.

Can't you hear the nightingale out in the fields
pour out melodies?

The breathing of the hills has filled
the sky, their breath
the scent of herbs

You need not fear, my love,
for never have the stars on high
told what they know.
Night's thick mists swirl in these vineyards;
they will veil our secrets.

You need not fear the spirit bride
will come out from
her magic cave.
She lies in drunken sleep, unseen by all
save houris' eyes.

The spirit king, if he should pass, let passion
give him due praise.
Like me he is in love and will not punish love,
for he burns too!

SONGS

In the depths of my soul there are songs unwilling to take the garb of words, songs living as seed in my heart. They will not flow with ink onto paper. Like a translucent veil, they are wrapped about emotions that can never flow sweetly on my tongue.

Yet how can I even whisper them when I fear what the particles of the æther may do to them? To whom shall I sing them when they have become accustomed to live in the house of my soul and fear the harshness of other ears?

Were you to look into my eye, you would see the image of their image. Were you to touch my fingertips, you would feel their quick movements.

The works of my hands reveal them as the lake reflects the twinkling of the stars. My tears disclose them as the mystery of the rose petal is disclosed at the moment the heat dissolves the drops of dew.

Songs spread out by silence and rolled up by noise, echoed in dreams and concealed by wakefulness.

They are songs of love, O people! What troubadour will sing them? What David shall chant these psalms?

More fragrant are they than the breaths of the jasmine flower. From what throat shall they go forth? More chaste are they than virgins. What violin will reveal them?

Who can combine the roaring of the sea and the warbling of the nightingale? Who can link the crashing thunder with the baby's sigh? What flesh can sing the songs of the gods?

Songs of the Wave

The shore and I are lovers, drawn together by desire and pulled apart by the wind. I come from beyond the blue dusk to mix the silver of my foam with the gold of his sand. I cool the heat of his heart with my mouth. At dawn I recite the law of passion into the ears of my lover, and he gathers me to his breast. In the evening I chant the prayer of longing, and he draws near.

I am importunate and uneasy; my lover is a patient comrade, a faithful friend.

As I rise, I embrace my lover. When the ebb follows, I throw myself upon his feet.

How often have I danced about the daughters of the sea when they rose from the depths and sat upon the rocks to delight in the sight of stars? How often have I heard the lover lament his passion for a lovely girl, and with him I have moaned and sighed? How often have I caroused with the rocks, though they are solid? Laughing I caressed them, yet they did not smile. How often have I rescued bodies from the chasms of the sea and carried them to the living? How often have I stolen pearls from the depths and given them to beautiful women?

In the silence of the night, when the phantoms of sleep have embraced all creatures, I watch, sometimes chanting, sometimes whispering. Woe is me, for watching by night has laid me waste. But I am a lover, and the essence of love is wakefulness.

This is my life, and that which is my life I must do.

SONGS OF THE RAIN

I am silver thread that the gods throw from on high. Nature seizes me and adorns the valleys.

I am lovely pearls fallen from Astarte's crown. The daughter of the morning stole them and studded the fields with them.

I weep, and the hills smile. I am abased, and the flowers hold high their heads. The cloud and the field are lovers, and I am that servant who goes between them. I weep and quench the thirst of the one and cure the disease of the other.

The crash of thunder and lightning swords herald my approach. The rainbow is the triumphal arch at my journey's end. This earthly life begins beneath the feet of angry matter and ends in the hands of peaceful death.

I rise from the heart of the lake and soar on ethereal wings. When I see a lovely garden, I descend and kiss its blossoms and embrace its branches.

In silence I drum my dainty fingertips upon the window glass, and that drumming blends into a song that perceptive souls can understand.

I am begotten by the heat of the air, yet I slay the air's heat. Thus may a woman master a man through power she draws from man.

I am the sighing of the sea. I am the tears of the sky. I am the smile of the field. So too is love a sigh from the sea of emotions, a tear from the sky of love, and a smile from the field of the soul.

Songs of Beauty

I am love's guide. I am the wine of the soul, the food of the heart. I am the flower that opened its heart when the day was young. A girl took me, kissed me, and placed me on her breast.

I am the house of felicity, the source of joy. I am the beginning of repose, the gentle smile on a maiden's lips. A youth sees me and forgets his companions. His life becomes a stage for dreams of pleasure.

I am the inspiration of poets, the guide of artists, the musician's teacher.

I am the gaze of the infant's eye. The loving mother sees it and bows in prayer and praise of God.

I appeared to Adam in the body of Eve and made him a slave. I appeared to Solomon in the figure of his beloved, and I made him sage and poet.

I smiled to Helen, and Troy was destroyed. I crowned Cleopatra, and love filled the valley of the Nile.

I, like time, build the day and raze its eve. I am God, bestowing life and death.

I am softer than the sigh of a violet's blossom, harsher than the storm. I am reality, O men.

I am reality, and I am goodness that you do not know.

Songs of Happiness

Man is my lover, and I am his beloved. I desire him, and he is inflamed by me. But, alas, I have a partner in his love who makes me wretched and torments him, a second wife named Matter who follows us wherever we go, a watcher keeping us apart.

I seek my lover in the countryside among the trees and by the lakes, but I do not find him. Matter has beguiled him and led him away to the city, to society and corruption and misery.

I seek him in the halls of knowledge and in the temples of wisdom, but I do not find him. Matter, she who is dressed in dust, has led him to the fortresses of selfishness where heedlessness dwells.

I seek him in the fields of contentment, but I do not find him, for my enemy has chained him in the caverns of gluttony and lust.

I call to him at dawn, when the east is filled with joy, but he does not hear me, for his eyes are heavy with the torpor of greed. I caress him in the evening when the darkness becomes silence and the flowers sleep, but he will not pay me heed, because he thinks only of the concerns of the morrow.

My lover loves me and seeks me in his own works, but he will find me only in the works of God. He seeks union with me in a palace of glory that he builds upon the skulls of the weak or in gold and silver. I will appear to him only in a simple house built by the gods on the banks of the emotions' stream. He seeks to kiss me before tyrants and murderers, but I will only allow him to taste of my mouth in solitude among the pure flowers. He would make deceit an intermediary between us, but I desire no intermediary save the stainless deed, the selfless act.

My lover has learned to cry and lament from my enemy, Matter; but I shall teach him to shed tears of entreaty from the eye of his soul and to sigh as he seeks contentment. My lover is mine, and I am his.

ROSE AL-HANI

I

I will tell you of an unhappy man who loved a girl. He took her as his life's companion, poured at her feet the sweat of his brow and the blood of his heart, placed in her open hands the fruits of his toil and the produce of his labor. He sought to buy her heart with days of toil and sleepless nights, but suddenly he found that she had given it to another man who would find pleasure in its hidden parts and delight in the secrets of its love.

I will tell you of an unhappy woman. She awoke from the thoughtlessness of youth to find herself in the house of a man who poured out his wealth as gifts to her, who clothed her in honor and affection, but who was unable to touch her heart with the spark of vivifying love, who could not intoxicate her spirit with that celestial wine that God pours from the eyes of a man into the heart of a woman.

I had known Rasheed Bey Nu'man since my childhood. His family had come from Mount Lebanon, but he was born and lived in Beirut. He was descended from an old and wealthy family that cherished the memory of its past glories. He was fond of retelling the stories that bespoke the nobility of his ancestors. He followed their ways and beliefs, preferring to follow them rather than the Western fashions that had begun to fill the sky of the East like flocks of birds.

Rasheed Bey was kind-hearted and generous in character but, like many of the people living in Syria, he did not look beyond things and saw only what was apparent. He did not listen to the song of his soul, but busied his affections with the songs produced by his surroundings. He was inclined to amuse himself with those tawdry things of the visible world that blind one to the secrets of life and that turn the soul away from apprehending the mysteries of being and toward the contemplation of temporal pleasures. He was one of those men who are in a hurry to show their love or hatred for people and things but then regret their haste after some time has passed, making them the butt of mockery and scorn, not forgiveness.

Such were the qualities and character of Rasheed Bey Nu'man that had led to his marrying Mistress Rose al-Hani before her soul had been bound to his under the shadow of the true love that makes married life a paradise.

I had been away from Beirut for a number of years, so when I returned I went to visit Rasheed. I found him sickly and pale. Ghosts of sorrows flickered in his features. The sorrowful looks that came from his eyes spoke silently of his bruised heart and the darkness within him. After looking around and seeing nothing to explain his emaciation and dejection, I asked him, "What has happened to you, sir? Where is the smile that used to shine on your face? Where has the happiness gone that was the constant companion of your youth? Has death come between you and a dear friend, or have the dark nights robbed you of the wealth which you gathered in the bright day? As a friend I ask you, what is this grief that has embraced your soul, this emaciation that rules your body?"

He gave me a regretful glance, for memory showed him images of days of beauty now veiled. In a voice whose trembling told of despair and hopelessness he said, "If a man loses a dear friend, he looks around and sees many friends come to console and comfort him. If a man loses his wealth, after a little thought he will realize that the delight that came from wealth will be restored by finding more. Thus he forgets his loss and is consoled. But if a man's heart is deprived of peace, where will he find it again, how will he replace it?

"When death stretches out its hand and slaps you violently, no more than a day and a night will pass before you feel the touch of the fingers of life, and you will smile and rejoice. Fate may come to you in a moment of heedlessness and stare at you with great and terrifying eyes, seize your neck in a grip of iron, throw you violently to the ground, trample you beneath its iron feet, and go away laughing. But soon it returns to you repentant, seeking forgiveness, gathering you up with silken hands, singing to you a hymn of hope, and filling you with song.

"Many afflictions and agonizing hardships may come to you, but the phantoms of the night will melt away with the coming of the morn, and you will feel your resolve clinging to your hopes. But if your portion of existence is a bird that you love, if you feed it with the grains of your heart, give it to drink from the light of your eyes, make your ribs to be its cage and your inner being its nest—then, if while you are looking at your bird and bathing its feathers with the rays of your soul, it flees from you and flies away circling above the clouds, if it then descends into another nest and there is no way to make it return. . . what then, sir, would you do? Tell me what you would do and where you would find patience and consolation, how you would revive your hopes and aspirations?"

Rasheed Bey spoke these last words in a choked and agonized voice. As he stood, he shook like a reed blown in the wind and reached forward as though he wanted to grab something with the fingers of his twisted hands and tear it to pieces. The blood rose to his face, darkening his wrinkled skin. He glowered, and his eyes hardened, and he stared for a moment as though he saw a demon before him, burst forth out of nothingness to bring him death. Then he looked back at me and his features quickly changed. The fury in his body became pain and torment. Weeping, he said, "She is the woman—the woman whom I delivered from the bondage of poverty and to whom I opened the doors of my treasuries. With fine clothes and costly ornaments, stately carriages and proud horses, I made her the envy of women. The woman whom my heart loved, at whose feet I poured my affections, to whom my soul was devoted, whom I drowned in generosity and gifts— the woman to whom I was an affectionate friend, a faithful companion, a loyal husband—she has betrayed me and left me! She has gone to the house of another man to live with him in the shadows of poverty. With him she shares bread dipped in disgrace and drinks water tainted with degradation and shame. The woman whom I loved, the beautiful bird whom I fed with grains of my heart and gave to drink from the light of my eyes, for whom my ribs were a cage and my inner being a nest, has fled from me and flown to another nest, a nest woven from the twigs of the thorn tree, there to eat thistles and maggots washed down with bitter poison! That pure angel whom I made to dwell in the paradise of my love and affection has become a demon fallen into the darkness to be tormented for her sins and to torment me with her crime!"

The man fell silent and covered his face with his hands as though trying to protect himself from himself. Then he sighed, "This is all that I am able to say. Don't ask me any more, and do not mention my affliction aloud. Rather, leave it to be a mute affliction. Perhaps it will grow in silence and kill me and give me peace."

I rose from my place, tears flowing from my eyes and sympathy grinding my heart. I departed from him in silence, for I could find no words that would solace his wounded heart and no wise counsel that would brighten his dark soul.

II

A few days later I met Mistress Rose al-Hani for the first time, in a humble house surrounded by flowers and trees. She had heard my name while she was in the house of Rasheed Bey Nu'man, that man whose

21

heart she had trampled and left for dead. When I saw her bright eyes and heard the song of her gentle voice, I said within myself, "Could this woman be capable of evil? Could such a transparent face mask a vile soul or the heart of a criminal? Is this the unfaithful woman? Is this the woman whom I have damned in my thought many times as a deadly viper concealed within the body of a graceful bird?" But on further thought I whispered to myself, "What else, then, besides this lovely face could have made that man so wretched? Have we not heard and seen that often superficial beauty has been the cause of hidden and dreadful afflictions, of deep and painful sorrows? Is not the moon, whose rays shine on limpid waters for the poets, that same moon that causes the ebb and flow of the tides troubling the seas?"

When I sat down, Mistress Rose sat with me, seeming to hear my thoughts and not wanting to prolong the struggle between my bewilderment and my doubts. Leaning her lovely head on her white hand, she spoke in a voice like the gentle reed flute, "I have not met you before, sir. But I have heard the echo of your thoughts and dreams in the mouths of men, so I know that you are sympathetic to the wronged woman, that you are merciful in her weakness, that you understand her emotions and desires. For that reason, I want to open my heart to you and show you what I have concealed within me, so that you will know the pain in my heart and will, if you desire, tell the people that

Rose al-Hani is not a wicked and unfaithful woman.

"When I was eighteen, fate led me to Rasheed Bey Nu'man. At that time he was nearly forty. He fell in love with me and treated me honorably, as people say. He made me his wife and the mistress of his splendid house and its many servants. He dressed me in silk and adorned my head and neck and wrists with jewelry and precious stones. He displayed me in the houses of his friends and acquaintances like some fine gift. He smiled with pride and triumph whenever his peers stared at me with envious pleasure. He raised his head proudly whenever he heard his friends' wives praise me or mention me with affection. But he did not hear the one who asked, 'Is this the wife of Rasheed Bey or his ward whom he has adopted?' And another said, 'If Rasheed Bey had married when he was young, his daughter would be older than Rose al-Hani.'

"All that took place before I had awakened from the deep sleep of childhood, before the gods had kindled the spark of love in my heart, before the seeds of emotion and desire sown in my heart had begun to grow. Truly, all of that happened in a time when I still imagined that the ultimate happiness was to wear a beautiful dress that flattered my figure, to ride in a stately carriage, to dress in costly fabrics.

"But when I awoke, aroused by light shining into my eyes, I felt tongues of sacred fire charring and consuming my ribs. As soon as I had awakened, I felt a spiritual hunger gripping and tormenting my soul. I saw my wings flexing on my right and on my left, seeking to bear me up into a heaven of love. But then they trembled and drooped, unable to break the chains of law. My body had been shackled before I had known the essence of those chains or the consequences of that law. When I awoke and felt these things, I knew that a woman's happiness is not to be found in a man's wealth or in obedience to him, nor even in his generosity and kindness. It is to be found in the love that binds her spirit to his, a love that pours her emotions into his heart, that makes them one limb of the body of life, one word upon the lips of God.

"When this painful truth had become clear to my sight, I felt like a thief in Rasheed Nu'man's house, eating his bread and then lurking in the darkness of the night. I knew that every day I spent near him was a ghastly lie, a lie that hypocrisy wrote in letters of fire upon my brow for heaven and earth to read, for I could not give him the love of my heart in return for his generosity, nor could I bestow the affection of my soul upon him in payment for his sincerity and goodness. I tried, futilely I tried to learn to love him, but I could not, for love is a power that creates our hearts. Our hearts cannot create love. Then I prayed and bowed before heaven in the silence of the night. My supplications and prayers could not engender a spiritual affection in the depths of my heart to draw me near to the man whom heaven had chosen as my companion. Love descends into our spirits by a decree of God, not by human intention. Thus, for two long years I remained in that man's house, envying the meadow larks their freedom, though the daughters of my own kind envied me for the prison in which I lived. Like a mother whose only child has died, I mourned the heart that had been conceived by knowledge, that had been sickened by law, and that died every day of hunger and thirst.

"On one of those black days, I stared from behind the darkness and beheld a diaphanous ray of light shining from my eye upon a youth walking alone on the paths of life, a youth who lived alone with his papers and books in this small house. I shut my eyes so as not to see that ray and said to my soul, 'Your lot is the darkness of the tomb. Do not covet the light!' Then I cried out and heard an exalted song, a song whose sweetness made my limbs tremble and whose purity seized my whole being. I covered my ears and said to my soul, 'Your lot is the hellfire that roars in your ears. Do not desire song!' I closed my eyes so as not to see and I blocked my ears so as not to hear, but my eyes still saw that ray, though they were closed, and my ears still heard that song, though blocked. At first I felt the terror of the poor man who finds a jewel near the palace of the prince. In his fear he dares not pick it up, yet his poverty will not let him leave it. I wept like a thirsty man who has seen a sweet spring guarded by wild beasts and who throws himself on the ground to wait and despair."

Mistress Rose fell silent for a moment and closed her eyes. The past stood before her, and she dared not look me in the face. Once again she spoke: "Some people come forth from eternity and then return to it without having tasted of true life. They cannot apprehend the essence of a woman's pain when her soul stands between the man she loves by the decree of heaven and the man to whom she is bound by earthly law. It is a tragedy written with a woman's blood and tears, but a man reads it as comedy because he does not understand it. And should he come to understand it, his laughter becomes debauchery and cruelty. His anger pours down upon the woman's head like the fires of hell, and he fills her ears with blasphemy.

"It is a story of pain. Dark nights act it out within the breast of the woman who finds her body chained to the bed of a man she knew as a husband before ever she knew the meaning of marriage. She sees her spirit fluttering around another man whom she loves with all the love that is within her spirit and with all the purity and beauty that is within love. It is a fearful struggle that began when weakness began in woman and strength in man. It will not end until the days of the servitude of weakness to strength have ended. It is a terrifying war between the corrupt laws of men and the sacred affections of the heart. Yesterday I was driven into this battlefield and nearly died of fear, nearly melted away in tears, but I stood up and cast off the timidity of the daughters of my kind. I freed my wings from the bonds of weakness and submission and rose in flight through the air of love and freedom. Now I am happy, near this man. He and I came out from the hand of God as a single spark before the ages began. There is no power in the world able to deny my happiness, for it arose from the embrace of two spirits linked by mutual understanding and overshadowed by love."

Mistress Rose looked at me thoughtfully as though her eyes could tear open my breast to see the affect of her words on my emotions and hear the echo of her voice within me. I remained silent lest I stop her from talking. Once again she spoke, now in a voice balanced between the bitterness of memory and the sweetness of emancipation and freedom.

"People will tell you that Rose al-Hani is an unfaithful and treacherous woman who followed the lust in her heart, that she abandoned the man who raised her up to be the mistress of his house. They will tell you that she is an adulterous whore whose polluted hands destroyed the holy diadem of marriage woven for her by religion, that she has taken in its place a filthy crown woven of thorns of hellfire. She has stripped the robe of virtue from her body and put on the clothes of sin and dishonor. They will tell you even

more than that, for the ghosts of their ancestors still
live in their bodies. They are like empty caves in the
valleys, returning the echoes of voices, not understand-
ing their meaning. They do not know the law of God
in his creatures. They do not understand the true sig-
nificance of religion. They do not know when man is
astray or righteous. With their small eyes they look
upon the exterior of acts but do not see their myster-
ies. In ignorance they judge and in blindness they
condemn. The guilty and the innocent, the righteous
and the wicked, are the same to them.

"Woe to him who judges, and woe to him who
condemns! It was in the house of Rasheed Nu'man that
I was an adulteress and unfaithful. He made me his
bed-partner by decree of custom and tradition, but
heaven had not made me his mate by the law of the
spirit and affection. Good things he gave me that he
might satisfy his desires in my body. Whenever I filled
my stomach from them, I was polluted and defiled
before my soul and before God. Now I have become
pure and chaste, for the law of love has set me free.
Now I am good and faithful, for I have renounced sell-
ing my body for bread and my days for raiment. Indeed,
I was an adulteress and a criminal when the people
reckoned me a virtuous wife. Today I have become pure
and good, yet they consider me a defiled whore. They
judge souls by the standards of bodies and weigh the
spirit in material scales."

Mistress Rose looked toward the window and pointed with her left hand at the city. Her voice, higher than before, was tinged with disgust and repugnance, as though among the alleys, on the roofs and porches she saw the ghosts of sin and degradation. "Look at these beautiful houses and tall and stately palaces. There live the rich and powerful among men. Their walls are decorated with silken tapestries yet enclose coarse treachery concealed by hypocrisy. Beneath their gilded roofs, falsehood stands close by affectation. Look! and think on those edifices with care. To you they symbolize wealth, power, and happiness, but they are no more than caves in which lurk degradation, misery, and wretchedness. They are whitewashed sepulchres in which the seduction of helpless women is concealed behind eyes darkened with kohl and reddened lips. Within them the flash of silver and gold hides the egotism and bestiality of men. They are palaces whose walls rise in haughtiness and pride toward the sky, but if they could perceive the stench of the loathsome things and deceit flowing from them, they would crumble and fall to the ground in ruin. The poor villager looks at them with tears in his eyes, yet within the hearts of their inhabitants no trace can be found of that sweet love filling the heart of that villager's wife. If he knew, he would smile in scorn and return to his field."

Mistress Rose took my hand and led me to the window overlooking those houses and palaces. "Come.

I will show you the secrets of these people, for I do not wish to be like them. Look at the palace with the marble pillars, ornamented with crystal windowpanes and copper. A rich man lives there. He inherited his wealth from his miserly father. His character he acquired in the street, where he learned all its vices. Two years ago he married a woman about whom he knew nothing save that her father had a hereditary position and a high rank among the elite of the city. The honeymoon had scarcely ended when he became bored and annoyed with her and once again began spending his nights with loose women. He left her in his palace as a drunkard leaves behind an empty wine jar. At first she wept and suffered. Then she learned patience, finding the consolation given the one who has recognized her mistake and knows that her tears are too precious to be spilled for the loss of a man such as her husband. Now she is preoccupied with a passion for a handsome and fair-spoken youth, pouring the yearning of her heart into his hands and filling his pockets with her husband's gold—a husband who no longer looks at her, as she no longer looks at him.

"Now look at that house surrounded by a lush garden. It is the home of a man born to a noble family that long governed the country. Now their station is lower. Their wealth has been dispersed and their sons are idle and lazy. Some years ago this man married. Though the girl was ugly, she was very rich. After he had gotten possession of her immense wealth, he forgot her existence and took a pretty mistress, leaving his wife to bite her nails in regret and waste away in longing. Now she spends her time pleating her hair, darkening her eyes, coloring her face with powders and creams, and adorning her body with satin and silk. She hopes that some visitor will look on her with favor, but no stares come her way save from the mirror.

"Then look at that great house adorned with murals and statues. It is the house of a woman whose face is beautiful but whose soul is foul. Her first husband died, and she inherited his wealth and estates. She chose a man weak of body and will to be her husband. His name protects her from people's tongues, and his presence defends her from accusations. Now she is like a bee among her admirers, sucking what is sweet and pleasurable from each flower.

"And look at that house, the one with wide porches and fine arches. It is the home of a man with material inclinations, with many business interests. He has a wife fair and comely in every part of her body, her spirit all sweetness and refinement. In the constitution of her person the elements of the soul are mingled with the delicacy of the body just as poetry combines the melody of meter with subtlety of meaning. She was formed to live by love and die by love, yet like most of the daughters of her sex, her father wronged her before she reached the age of eighteen and placed her neck in the yoke of a sinful marriage. Now her body is emaciated, melting like wax in the heat of her chained affections. It slowly disappears like a fair wind before a storm. She is being destroyed by a love for something beautiful which she can sense but cannot see. She yearns, longs for the embrace of death to emancipate her from her harsh life, to free her from a man who spends his days gathering gold and his nights counting it, who grinds his teeth cursing the hour in which he married a barren woman who could not bear him a son to carry on his name and inherit his wealth and treasures.

"Look at the house standing alone among the orchards. It is the home of a poet, imaginative and high-minded, spiritual in his religion. He has a wife, coarse of mind and common. She mocks his poems because she does not understand them. She belittles his actions because they are eccentric. Now he ignores her, having fallen in love with a married woman. This woman has a fiery intelligence and flows with grace. Her love has brightened his heart. She inspires his immortal words with her smiles and loving glances."

Mistress Rose fell silent for a moment. She was sitting in a seat by the window, her soul seemingly wearied by roaming the bedchambers of those secret houses. Then she slowly began to speak again: "These palaces—I did not wish to be among their inhabitants. They are graves: I did not wish to be buried alive among these sepulchres. These people—I have been emancipated from their customs. The yoke of their society has been lifted from me. These are the married people who are wedded in body yet loathe each other in spirit. Nothing will intercede for them before God save their own ignorance of the law of God. I do not condemn them now; rather, I pity them. I do not hate them; rather, I hate their thoughtless submission to hypocrisy, falsehood, and evil. I do not tell you the secrets of their hearts and of their lives because I like gossip and slander. Rather, I do this to show you the truth about a people. Only yesterday I was no different than them, yet I was saved. I am explaining to you the way of life of a people who say every sort of wicked thing about me because I sacrificed their friendship to gain my own soul. I left the dark paths of their duplicity and turned my eyes toward the light where there is salvation, truth, and justice. They have exiled me now from their society, yet I am content. Mankind only exiles the one whose large spirit rebels against injustice and tyranny. He who does not prefer exile to servility is not free in the true and necessary sense of freedom. Yesterday I was like an inviting table, and Rasheed Bey would come to me whenever he felt a need to taste of it, but our souls remained far apart like two lowly servants. When I comprehended this knowledge, I hated the servitude. Though I tried to submit to what they call 'my lot,' I could not. My spirit refused to spend all of life bowing before a fearful idol raised by dark generations of the past, an idol which they made law. So I broke my bonds, but I did not cast them away until I heard love calling and saw my soul prepared for a journey.

"I left the house of Rasheed Nu'man like a prisoner freed from his prison, leaving behind me jewelry, clothing, servants, and carriages. I came to my beloved's house, a place empty of ornaments but full of spirit. I know that I have done nothing that was not right and obligatory, for heaven did not will that I should cut off my wings with my own hand and throw myself into the ashes, hiding my head in my arms, pouring out the last of my life with my tears, while saying, 'This is my lot in life.' Heaven does not wish me to spend my life crying out in pain in the nights, saying, 'When will the dawn come?' Yet when the dawn came, I would say, 'When will this day end?' Heaven did not wish man to be unhappy, for it has placed in the depths of his being a longing for happiness—for through man's happiness God is glorified.

"This is my story, O man. This is my justification before heaven and earth. I repeat it, I sing it out, but men block their ears and do not hear, for they fear revolution in their spirits, they fear that the pillars of their society will be shaken and it will fall upon their heads.

"This is the difficult path that I travel to reach the summit of my happiness. If death should come now and snatch me away, my spirit will stand before the high throne without fear or dread—indeed, with joy and hope. My conscience will be unwrapped before the Most Great Judge and it will be seen to be pure as snow, for I have done nothing that was not willed by a soul that God split off from His own Self. I have followed only the call of the heart and the echo of the angels' song.

"This is my story, a story that the people of Beirut consider to be a curse in the mouth of life, a disease in the body of society. They will find regret when the days finally awaken the love of love in their dark hearts as the sun brings forth flowers from the midst of the earth, though the earth is filled with the remains of the dead. Then the passerby will stand by my tomb and greet it saying, 'Here lies Rose al-Hani, who freed her affections from servitude to corrupt human laws to live by the law of a noble love. She turned her face so as not to see her shadow among the skulls and thorns.' "

Mistress Rose only stopped speaking when the door opened and a slender young man with a handsome face came in. A magical light shone from his eyes and a slight smile was on his lips. Mistress Rose stood and took his arm with complete affection. She introduced him to me, mentioning my name courteously and his name with a significant look. Thus I knew that he was the youth for whom she had renounced the world and defied laws and conventions.

We sat down in silence, for each of us wished to ascertain what the other thought of him. A minute passed, a minute filled with that silence which turns souls toward the heavenly hosts. I looked at them sitting next to each other and saw something that I had not seen before. In a glance I understood the meaning of the story of Mistress Rose. I apprehended the mystery of her rejection of a social order that condemns those who rebel against its laws before it investigates the reasons for their rebellion. Before me I saw a single celestial spirit in two bodies, handsome in their youth and clothed in union. The god of love stood between them, spreading his wings to shelter them from people's criticism and censure. I found total mutual understanding shining from two luminous faces made bright by sincerity, bathed in purity. For the first time in my life, I saw the vision of happiness raised between a man and a woman who had been repudiated by religion and driven out by the law.

After a moment I stood up and bade them farewell. Without my speaking, the degree to which my soul had been stirred was apparent to them. I left that humble house, a house that emotions had made a temple of love and affection. As I walked among the palaces and estates whose secrets Mistress Rose had revealed to me, I pondered her conversation and all the beginnings and endings entwined within it. But before I reached the boundary of that quarter, I remembered Rasheed Bey Nu'man and saw once more the agony of his despair and unhappiness. I thought, "He is a wronged and wretched man, but does heaven hear him if he stands before it wronged and complaining of Rose al-Hani? Did that woman sin against him when she left him and followed her own freedom? Or was he the one who sinned against her when he subjugated her body by marriage before her spirit inclined itself toward love? Which of the two is the wrongdoer and which the one wronged? Which would you say is guilty and which innocent?"

Then I once again pondered events past, reviewing them in my mind: "How often has vanity seduced women into leaving poor men and attaching themselves to rich men, for the craving that women have for fine clothes and luxury blinds them and leads them to dishonor and degradation. But was Rose al-Hani deceived by vanity and covetousness when she left the palace of a rich man, a palace packed with ornaments, fine clothing, and servants, to go to a poor man's hut containing nothing but a shelf of old books? How often has ignorance killed the honor of a woman and revived her passions so that she abandoned her husband out of boredom and spite and sought the pleasures of the body with another man more debased and less honorable than her? Was Rose al-Hani ignorant, did she desire only the pleasures of the body when she openly proclaimed her independence before witnesses and attached herself to a youth of spiritual inclinations? In her husband's house she might have sated her desires in secret with besotted young men willing to destroy themselves as slaves to her beauty, as martyrs to their lust for her. Rose al-Hani was an unhappy woman who sought happiness, who found it, who embraced it. This is the truth that human society despises and the law denies."

I whispered these words into the ears of the æther, then asked myself, "But is it permissible for a woman to make her husband's misery the price of her happiness?" My own soul answered me, "Is it allowable for a man to enslave his wife's affections for his own happiness?"

I kept on walking with the voice of Mistress Rose echoing in my ears. When I reached the edge of the city, the sun was setting on the fields as the orchards put on the veil of silence and repose and the birds chanted the evening prayer. I stood in thought, then whispered, "Before the throne of freedom these trees rejoice in their dalliance with the breeze. Before its majesty they take pleasure in the rays of the sun and moon. The sparrows sing their secrets in the ears of freedom, and along the streams they flutter about the hems of its robe. The flowers pour their perfumed breaths into the air of freedom, and they smile before its eyes at the coming of the morn. All that is on the earth lives by the law of its nature. From the nature of its law it seeks the splendor and the delights of freedom. But men are forbidden this goodness because they have entrusted their divine spirits to a worldly and limited law. They have subjected their bodies and souls to a single harsh law. For their desires and emotions they have raised a narrow and frightful prison, and for their hearts and minds they have dug a deep and gloomy grave. Whenever one arises among them and sets himself apart from their society and laws, they say, 'This is a wicked rebel, worthy of banishment, a defiled sinner who merits death.' But is man to continue a slave to his corrupt laws until the end of the ages, or will time free him to live by the spirit and for the spirit? Will man continue to stare at the dust, or will he turn his eyes toward the sun so as not to see his shadow among the thorns and skulls?"

THE ENCHANTING SPIRIT

*E*nchantress, where are you leading me?

Where am I following you on this rough path twisting among the rocks? On this path covered with thorns we climb on foot toward the mountain peaks and descend alone into the depths.

I cling to your hem and follow behind you like a child clinging to his mother, forgetting my own dreams and staring at the beauty that is in you. I blind myself to the processions of phantoms circling about my head, enraptured by the hidden power concealed within your body.

Wait beside me awhile, and I will look into your face. Look at me for a moment so that in your eyes I might see the mysteries of your heart, might understand from your features those things hidden in your soul.

Spirit, wait a little while, for I am weary of the path and my soul trembles at the terrors of the road.

Wait, for we have reached that crossroads where death embraces life. I will not go another step until you plainly tell my soul the intentions of your soul, until you disclose to my heart what lies treasured in your heart.

Listen to me, enchanting Spirit!

Yesterday I was free, soaring among the brooks and swimming in the sky. In the evenings I would sit on the highest branches, seeing castles and palaces in a city of colored clouds, a city built by the sun in an afternoon and destroyed before nightfall.

No, I was like a thought traveling alone through the east and west of the world, joyous in the good things and pleasures of life, delving deeply into the hidden secrets and mysteries of being.

I was like a dream striving beneath the dark of night. Through the slits of windows I entered the chambers of sleeping virgins, playing with their emotions. Then would I stand by the navels of youths and excite their desires. I would sit near the couches of old men and discover their hidden thoughts.

Today, enchantress, I met you and was poisoned by the kisses of your hand. I rose like a prisoner dragging my chains toward I know not what. It was as though I were intoxicated, seeking more of the wine that had stolen my will and kissing the palm of the hand that had slapped me.

But stop a little, enchantress, have I taken back my faculties and broken the fetters that wearied my feet? Have I smashed the cup from which I drank the poison that seemed so sweet to me. What do you wish me to do? Which path do you wish us to travel?

I ask for my freedom back. Will you be content with a free companion? "Can you stare at the face of the sun with open eyes or grasp the fire with steady hands?"

I have opened my wings a second time. Will you be the companion of a youth soaring like an eagle among the mountains, or like a lion passing the nights resting in the wilderness?

Will you be satisfied with the love of a man who has taken love as a friend but will not let it be his lord?

Will the passion of a heart suffice you, a heart enraptured but unwilling to surrender, that burns but will not melt?

Will you find peace with the affections of a soul that trembles before the storm but does not break, that shakes in the tempest but is not uprooted?

Will you be content with me as a companion, a companion who will seek to be neither master nor slave?

If so, here is my hand. Take it in your fair hand. Here is my body. Embrace it with your lovely arms. Here is my mouth. Kiss it with a long, deep, silent kiss.

THE LIFE OF LOVE

SPRING

*C*ome, my beloved, let us walk among the ruins, for the snows have melted. Life stirs from its couch and swirls among the valleys and hills. Go with me and we will trace the footsteps of spring in the distant field. Come, let us go up to the hilltops and see the plains in waves of green around us.

For spring has unfolded the garment that the winter night had rolled up. The plum tree and the apple wear it, arrayed like brides on the Holy Night. The orchards have shaken off their slumber. Their branches embrace like crowds of lovers. The streams flow, dancing among the stones, echoing songs of joy. Flowers burst from the heart of nature like froth on the sea.

Come, let us drink the last raindrop tears from a narcissus cup and fill our souls with the songs of larks.

Now is our time to breath deeply of the scent of spring breezes.

Let us sit by the stone where the violet is hidden, exchanging kisses of love.

SUMMER

Come, let us go to the field, for the days of the harvest have come. The crop is now grown, and the heat of the sun's love for nature has ripened it. Come, before the birds forestall us and reap the fruits of our toil, or before a colony of ants takes our land. Come, let us reap the fruits of the soil, as the soul reaps the fruits of happiness grown from the seeds of fidelity—seeds planted by love in the depths of our two hearts. Let us fill storehouses with the products of the elements, even as life fills up the granaries of our emotions.

Come, my companion, let us lie upon the grass with heaven as our blanket. Let us lay our heads upon fresh hay and rest from the labor of the day, listening to the night whispers of the brook in the valley below.

AUTUMN

Let us go to the vineyard, my beloved, and press the grapes, filling the vats with juice as the soul is filled with the wisdom of generations. Let us gather the dried fruits and distill the blossoms, sacrificing the flower itself to preserve its lingering scent.

Let us return to the dwellings, for the leaves of the trees are now brown and scatter before the wind. The wind will make them a shroud for flowers dead in their longing for the summer that has forsaken them. Let us go, for the birds have journeyed toward the shore, carrying with them the friendliness of the meadows and leaving behind in desolation the jasmine and the myrtle to weep their last tears onto the ground.

Let us go back, for the brooks have ceased to flow. The springs have dried their tears of joy. The hills are stripped of their splendid robes. Come, my beloved, for nature is seduced by lethargy and says its evening farewells to wakefulness in the plaintive strains of Nihavand.

WINTER

Come near, my life's companion. Come near to me, and do not let the icy breaths separate our two bodies. Sit beside me before the hearth, for fire is the sweetest fruit of winter. Tell me stories of bygone times, for my ears weary of the wind's sighs and the keening of the elements. Bolt the doors and windows, for the sight of angry weather saddens my soul and the sight of the town, sitting like a bereaved mother beneath layers of ice, oppresses my heart. . . Fill the lamp with oil, O my life's companion, for it burns low. Place it near me so I can see what the nights have written on your face.

Bring a jug of wine for us to drink, and we will remember the days when it was pressed.

Come, come near to me, beloved of my soul, for the fire has burned down and the ashes cover it. Embrace me, for the lamp has gone out and darkness presses in. Our eyes have grown heavy with the wine of years. Look on me with eyes shadowed with sleep. Embrace me before slumber embraces me. Kiss me, for the ice has conquered all but your kiss. And oh, my beloved, how deep is the sea of sleep, how far distant is the morning. . . in this world!

In a Year Unrecorded in History

*I*n the shade of the walnut and willow trees, the peasant's son sat on the riverbank watching the water flow slowly and silently past. He was a youth educated in the fields, where everything spoke of love—where trees embraced, where flowers reached out to each other, where birds sang of their love, where nature in its entirety preached the spirit. He was twenty years old. Yesterday he had seen a girl sitting among the young women at the spring and had fallen in love with her. But then he had learned that she was the daughter of the Emir, and he had reproached his heart, and his soul complained to itself within him. Yet complaint does not turn the heart from love, nor does rebuke turn the soul away from reality. Man caught between his heart and soul is like a thin branch whipping between the north wind and the south.

The youth saw a violet growing near a daisy. He heard a nightingale singing to a thrush, and he wept in his loneliness. The hours of his love passed before his eyes like phantoms. His emotions poured out with his words and his tears:

"See how love mocks me! Will it make a joke of me and lead me to a place where hopes become sins and longings shame? Love, whom I have worshipped, has lifted up my heart to the Emir's palace and brought down my station to a peasant's hut. It has led my soul to a ravishing houri, to one surrounded by noblemen and guarded by an aristocrat's honor. Love, I am obedient, but what would you have me do? Your paths led through the fire, and the flames scorched me. I opened my eyes, but I saw only darkness. I loosed my tongue, but I spoke only of grief. Longing has embraced me, O Love, with a spiritual hunger that can only be sated with the beloved's kiss. I am weak, O Love, so why must you, who are strong, oppose me? Why do you wrong me when you are just and I am innocent? Why do you abase me when I have no other helper but you? Why do you forsake me, though you are my creator? If my blood has flowed in my veins against your will, then shed it! If my feet have walked any paths but yours, then make them wither! Do what you will with this body, but leave my soul to rejoice in safety in these fields beneath the shadow of your wings. The brooks flow to their lover, the sea, and the flowers smile at the object of their passion, the light. The mist rolls down to its beloved, the valley. And I? In me is what brooks do not know, what flowers do not hear, what the mist does not apprehend. You see me alone in my love, solitary in my yearning, far away from her. She does not want me even as a soldier in her father's regiments, does not think me worthy to be a servant in her palace."

The youth was silent for a moment, as though he sought to learn the language of the rippling river and the rustling leaves. Then once again he spoke:

"O you whose name makes me dread to call your name, O you who are concealed from me by veils of greatness and walls of glory, houri whom I cannot hope to meet save in the equality of eternity. O you whom strong men obey, before whom servants bow low, to whom treasuries and temples are open, you rule a heart sanctified by love and have won the worship of a soul made noble by God. You have bewitched a mind that yesterday possessed the freedom of the fields but today has become a prisoner in the bonds of this passion. Fair one, I saw you and knew the reason I came into this world. When I learned how high was your station and considered my own lowliness, I understood that the gods have secrets not known to man, paths that spirits walk to a place where love shines without regard to human laws. I knew with certainty when I looked into your eyes that this life is a paradise whose gate is the human heart. When I saw your high rank and my own abasement wrestling like a lion and its prey, I knew that this world could no longer be my homeland. When I found you sitting among your la-dies-in-waiting like a rose among the grasses, I thought that the bride of my dreams had been made flesh like me. When I learned of the high rank of your father, I found that the price of plucking the rose is fingers bloodied on the thorns—that what dreams gather, wakefulness scatters."

He stood then and walked toward the spring, shoulders drooping, brokenhearted, giving voice to his grief and despair:

"Come, Death, deliver me! This earth, where thorns strangle the flowers, is not a fit place to live. Free me from this age in which love has been deposed from its throne of glory and high rank has usurped its place. Free me, Death, for eternity is a better place for lovers to meet than this world. There I will await my beloved, and there we will be united."

When he reached the spring, evening was falling. The sun began to remove its golden bands from the fields as he sat there. His tears fell onto the ground that the Emir's daughter had trod. He bent his head to his chest as if to prevent his heart from escaping.

At that moment a girl appeared from behind the willows, trailing her skirts in the grass. She stood beside the youth and placed her silken hand on his head. He looked at her, a sleeper wakened by a ray of sun. He saw the Emir's daughter standing beside him. He fell to his knees, as when Moses saw the Burning Bush before him. His voice shook too much to speak, but his eyes, wet with tears, spoke for him.

The girl embraced him and kissed his lips, drinking the hot tears. In a voice softer than the reed-flute's song, she said, "I saw you, my beloved, in dreams. I saw your face in my solitude and isolation. You are the companion of my soul who was lost, the fairer half of me that was separated when it was decreed I should come into this world. I have come in secret to meet you, my love. Now you are in my arms, so do not grieve. I have forsaken my father's wealth to follow you to the ends of the earth, to drink with you from the cup of life and death. Rise, my love! Let us go to a wilderness far from men."

The two lovers walked among the trees, hidden by the veils of night, fearing neither the wrath of the Emir nor the phantoms of the dark.

There, on the edges of the city, the Emir's scouts came upon two human skeletons. Around the neck of one was a golden necklace. Near them was a stone on which these words had been inscribed:

"Love has united us, so who can separate us? Death has taken us, so who can bring us back?"

THE BELOVED

FIRST SIGHT

*I*t is the moment dividing the scent of life from its wakefulness. It is the first spark lighting the recesses of the soul. It is that first magical note plucked on the strings of the lyre of the human heart. It is a brief moment retelling to the soul's ear tales of bygone days and revealing to its visions deeds done by night, making plain to its eye the acts of ecstasy in this world and the mystery of eternity in the world to come. It is a seed throw from on high by Astarte. The eyes sow it in the field of the heart, the emotions tend it, and the soul brings it to fruit. The first sight of the beloved is like the spirit that moved on the face of the waters, from which flowed forth the heavens and the earth. The first sight of life's companion echoes God's words, "Let there be. . . "

First Kiss

It is the first sip from a goblet that the gods have filled from the fountain of love. It is the boundary between a doubt that seduces and saddens the heart and a certitude that fills it with happiness. It is the opening line of the poem of spiritual life, the first chapter of the novel of astral man. It is the cord that binds the exile of the past to the splendor of the future. It unites the silence of the senses with their songs. It is a word spoken by four lips proclaiming the heart a throne, love a king, faithfulness a crown. It is a gentle touch telling how the fingers of the wind caressed the rose's mouth, carrying away a long sigh of pleasure and a sweet and quiet moan. It is the beginning of magical tremblings that separate the lovers from the world of space and dimensions and carry them to the world of revelation and dreams. It joins the anemone to the pomegranate blossom, mingling their two scents to create a third soul.

If the first sight is like a seed sown by the gods in the field of the human heart, the first kiss tells of the first flower blossoming on the twigs of the tree of life's first branch.

Union

Now love begins to make poetry of life's prose, to shape from past thoughts psalms to chant in the days and to sing in the nights. Now desire rips away the veils of

doubt from the riddles of past years. From tufts of pleasure it weaves a happiness surpassed only by the happiness of the soul when she embraces her lord. Union is the linking of two divinities to produce a third upon the earth. It is two strong individuals standing shoulder to shoulder to oppose with their love the malice of a weak fate. It is the mingling of a yellow wine with scarlet to produce a golden draught, the color of the horizon as dawn breaks. It is the aversion of two spirits to aversion and the unity of two souls with unity. It is a golden circle formed by a chain whose first link is a glance and whose last is infinity. It is the falling of a limpid rain from a pure sky upon the holiness of nature, bringing forth the powers of blessed fields.

If the first glance from the face of the beloved is like a seed sown by love in the field of the heart, and the first kiss from two lips is like the first flower on the branch of life, union is the first fruit of the first flower of that seed.

THE QUEEN
OF IMAGINATION

*W*hen I reached the ruins of Palmyra, I was weary from the journey. I lay down on the grass growing among pillars that time had uprooted and thrown to the ground. They appeared to be the dead of some awful war. I fell to pondering the great things which though in ruins and utterly destroyed are yet esteemed above that which still stands and lives.

When night came and the quarreling creatures consented to share one robe of silence, I became conscious of something flowing in the æther surrounding me. Its scent was like incense and its effect was like wine. I drank it uncontrollably. I felt unseen hands interfering with my reason, weighing down my eyelids, unlocking the chains that bound my soul. Then the earth shook, the sky trembled, and I jumped, compelled by a magical power. I found myself in a garden of beauty inconceivable to any man, surrounded by a choir of maidens clothed only in beauty. They walked about me, their feet not touching the grass, singing a hymn of praise spun from dreams of love. They played lutes made of ivory, with golden strings. I came to an open spot, in the midst of which rose a throne. It was encrusted with gems from which poured out light in all the colors of the rainbow. The maidens stopped to its right and its left and raised their voices higher than before. They looked in a direction from which came the scent of frankincense and myrrh. A queen appeared from among the flowering trees, walked slowly toward the throne, and mounted it. At that moment a flock of doves came down, as white as snow, and alighted in a crescent around her feet.

The doves and the maidens began to sing psalms to the greatness of the queen. Pillars of incense rose to glorify her. I stood watching what no man's eye had seen and hearing what no ear of flesh had heard.

Then the queen gestured with her hand. All movement ceased. She spoke in a voice that made my soul vibrate as the strings of the lute vibrate when touched by the musician's hand. It was as though in these magical surroundings all things had ears. "I called you, mortal man. I am the mistress of the theatres of imagination. I have granted you leave to stand before me. I am the queen of the forest of dreams. Listen to my counsels and proclaim them before mankind. Tell them that the city of imagination is a wedding feast, but its gate is barred by a giant demon who will allow only those to enter who wear finery for the feast. Tell them that it is a paradise guarded by the angel of love and no one will see it save those on whose brow is burned the brand of love. It is a meadow of fantasies, whose rivers are sweet as wine, whose birds sing like angels, whose air is fragrant with flowers—but only the son of dreams will walk in that meadow. Tell men that I have granted them a chalice overflowing with happiness, but they have spilled it in their ignorance. Now the angel of darkness has come and filled it with the distillation of sorrow. They have drained the cup and are drunk with it. Say that they cannot play the lyre of life with skill unless their fingertips have touched my belt and their eyes have gazed upon my throne.

"The verses of Isaiah were pearls of wisdom which he threaded upon the strings of my love. With my tongue John told of his vision. It was I who guided Dante through the realms of the spirits. I am a metaphor that embraces reality, a reality that reveals the unity of the soul, a witness who justifies the ways of the gods. Tell them that thought has a homeland more splendid that the world of visible things, a homeland whose sky is not obscured by clouds of happiness. Tell them that what they imagine is drawn in the sky of the gods and reflected upon the mirror of their souls. Thus may they hope for more when they are freed from this lower life."

The Queen of Imagination drew me toward her by a magical glance and kissed my flaming lips. "And tell them: whosoever does not spend his days in the theatre of dreams is a slave all his days."

At that the voices of the maidens grew louder, the pillars of incense rose, and the vision was concealed. Then the earth shook and the sky trembled and I found myself among those sad ruins. Dawn was smiling, but still between my tongue and lips were these words, "Whosoever does not spend his days in the theatre of dreams is a slave all his days."

WORDS OF LOVE

*I*n a lonely house a youth in the morning of his life sat staring sometimes out the window at a sky adorned with stars and sometimes at the picture of a girl before him. The lines and the colors of the picture were reflected in his face, revealing there the mysteries of this world and the secrets of eternity. The portrait of the woman's face spoke secretly to him, making his eyes into ears that understood the language of the spirits floating in the air of that room, turning his whole being into hearts bright with love and overflowing with longing.

An hour passed this way as though it were a moment in a pleasant dream or a year in eternity. Finally the youth placed the picture before him, picked up pen and paper, and wrote,

"Beloved of my soul!

"The great truths that are above nature do not pass from one human being to another by means of ordinary human speech. Rather, they choose silence as the path between souls. I know well that the silence of this night hastens between our souls bearing messages more subtle than the words written by the spring breeze on the face of the water. It recites the book of our two hearts to our two hearts. But just as God wills to imprison souls in bodies, it is the will of love to make me a prisoner of words. They say, Beloved, that love is transformed in its servants into a consuming fire. I have found that the hour of separation has been unable to divide the essence of our two spirits, just as I knew at our first meeting that my soul had known yours throughout the ages, just as I knew that my first sight of you was not in reality the first sight. Beloved! That hour bound together our two hearts, exiled from the higher world. That hour was one of those few hours that made firm my faith in the preexistence and immortality of the soul. In hours such as that nature unveils the face of its infinite justice, yet they think it to be tyranny.

"My Beloved, do you remember in that garden, each of us looking into the face of his lover? Do you know that your glances told me that your love for me did not spring from pity? Those glances told me that I could tell myself and all the world that the gift whose source is justice is greater than the gift from charity, that the love created by circumstances is like stagnant waters.

"Before me, my Beloved, is a life that I want to be great and beautiful, a life that will find its place in the memory of men to come, that will merit their respect and affection, a life that began when I met you. I am convinced that it is eternal, for I believe that you are able to manifest the power that God has entrusted to me. It is a power that I will embody in great words and deeds just as the sun makes the fragrant wildflowers to grow in the meadow. Thus shall my love continue for me and for generations to come, pure of the egotism that might extend it and exalted above the degradation that would restrict it to you."

The youth stood and walked slowly around that room. He looked out the window and saw the moon rising above the horizon and filling the sky with delicate rays. He came back and wrote in the letter:

"Forgive me, Beloved, for I have addressed you as 'you,' yet you are the fair half of me which I lost when we left the hand of God at the same moment. Forgive me, my Beloved."

COMMUNION

*W*here are you now, my fair one? Are you in that small garden watering the flowers that love you as the infant loves its mother's breast? Or are you in your chamber where you have built an altar to purity and sacrificed there my spirit and my last breath? Or are you among your books, increasing your knowledge of men's wisdom, though you have no need to seek wisdom even from the gods?

Where are you, companion of my soul? Are you in the temple praying for me? Or are you in the meadow, holding communion with nature, the source of your wonderment and dreams? Are you in the huts of the poor, comforting the broken-hearted with the sweetness of your soul and filling their hands with your charity?

You are everywhere, for you are from the spirit of God. You are in every time, for you are stronger than fate.

Do you remember the nights we were together, haloed in the rays of your soul, and the angels of love circled about us singing anthems of the spirit's deeds? Do you remember the days we sat shadowed by branches? They covered us like a tent to veil us from men as the ribs conceal the secrets of the saintly heart. Do you remember the paths and hills we walked together, your fingers entwined in mine like the twining of your hair? Our heads leaned upon each other as though we would protect ourselves from ourselves. Do you remember the hour when I came to bid you farewell? You embraced me, then kissed me. You gave me the kiss of Mary, and I knew that joined lips bear divine secrets that the tongue cannot know. A kiss is the preface to a two-fold sigh, telling the tale of the breath God blew into clay and thus made man. That sigh went before us to the world of the spirits, proclaiming the glory of our two souls. There it will remain until we are joined with it forever. Then you kissed me and kissed me, and you said, aided by a tear, "Bodies have purposes that we do not know. They are divided for worldly reasons and taken far apart for earthly ends. But spirits remain in the hand of love, safe until death comes and bears them away to God. Go, my lover, life has given you an order, so you must obey. It is gracious, giving the obedient overflowing cups to drink from the fountain of pleasure. As for me, your love will be a faithful bridegroom and your memory a long and blessed wedding feast."

Where are you now, my companion? Do you lie wakeful in the silence of the night? I have charged the breeze whenever it blows toward you to bear to you the beating of my heart and the secrets of my limbs. Or are you staring at the picture of your lover? That picture is no longer true, for sadness has cast its image upon a brow that yesterday was happy being near to you. Grief has dulled the eyes that once shone with your beauty. Longing has dried the lips that once were moist with your kisses.

Where are you, my beloved? Do you hear my call and my grief from beyond the seas? Do you see my weakness and misery? Do you know my patience and my endurance? Are there no spirits in the air who will transmit the agonized breaths of a dying man? Are there no invisible cords between souls to carry the lament of the lovesick lover?

Where are you, my life? Darkness has embraced me and grief overwhelmed me. Smile in the air, and I will be restored. Breath into the æther, and I will be revived.

Where are you, my beloved, where are you?

Ah, how great is love, and how small am I!

AMONG THE RUINS

*T*he moon laid a thin veil over the thickets surrounding Heliopolis, and calm took the reins of all beings. The fearful ruins appeared like giants mocking the vicissitudes of the nights.

In that hour two forms flowed out of nothingness, like vapors rising from an azure lake. On a marble column formed by time from that strange building, they sat contemplating their surroundings, surroundings that told of scenes of enchantment. After a while, one of them raised his head and spoke in a voice that sounded like an echo in the caves of distant valleys.

"These are the remains of temples I built for you, my beloved. Over there are the ruins of a castle I raised to please you. It has been pulled down and nothing remains but a trace to tell the nations of the glory that I spent my life to proclaim and the might that I compelled the weak to glorify. Consider, my beloved, how the elements have razed the city I built so strongly and how succeeding generations have belittled the philosophy that I held. Oblivion has surrounded the kingdom I made great, and nothing remains to me save the moments of love to which your beauty gave birth and the effects of the beauty to which your love gave life. I built a temple in Jerusalem for worship. The priests sanctified it, and the passing days crushed it. I built a temple within my breast. God sanctified it, and no force can overpower it. I poured out my life seeking the meaning of external things, explaining the actions of matter. Man says, "How wise a king you are!" The angels say, "How poor a sage he is!" Then I saw you, my beloved, and I sang you a hymn of love and yearning. The angels rejoiced, but man took no notice. The days of my reign were but barriers between my thirsty spirit and the fair spirit established in beings. When I saw you, love awoke, those barriers were torn down. I regretted the life I had squandered by yielding to rivers of despair and reckoning as vanity all things under the sun. I wove chain mail and hammered shields, and all the tribes feared me. When love illumined me, even my own people despised me. But when death came, it cast this chain mail and these shields in the dust, and my love bore me up to God."

After a silence, the second form replied, "Just as the flower takes its fragrance and its life from the dust, so too the soul acquires power and wisdom from the weakness and folly of matter."

At that the two forms intermingled as a single form and vanished. After a moment these words reverberated through the air around that place, "Only love will last through eternity, for they are alike."

BEFORE SUICIDE

*Y*esterday the woman whom my heart loved sat in this still and lonely room.

Yesterday she laid her lovely head on these soft flowered pillows. From this crystal cup she drank a mouthful of wine mixed with a drop of perfume.

All that was yesterday. Yesterday is a dream that will not return. Today the woman whom my heart loved has gone to an empty, bleak, and distant land, which they name the Land of Emptiness and Oblivion.

The marks of her fingers are still visible on the glass of my mirror. The perfume of her breath still scents the folds of my clothes. Her voice still echoes in the corners of my house. But the woman herself—the woman whom my heart loved—has traveled to a distant place called the Valley of Exile and Forgetting. The marks of her fingers, the perfume of her breath, the phantoms of her spirit will linger in this room until tomorrow morn. Then I will open the windows of my house to let in streams of air to sweep away all that that beautiful sorceress left behind for me.

The portrait of the woman my heart loved still hangs beside my bed. The love letters she sent me are still in the silver box, encrusted with agate and coral. The lock of golden hair she gave me is still in the silk pouch full of musk and frankincense. All these things will stay in their places until morning. When morning comes, I will open the windows of my house to let the air carry away the darkness of non-being to a place where dumb silence dwells.

The woman whom my heart loved is like the women you young men love. She is an astonishing creature shaped by the gods from the gentleness of the dove, the fickleness of the asp, the pride of the peacock, the malice of the wolf, the beauty of the white rose, the terror of the dark night, mixed with a handful of ashes and the foam of the sea.

I had known the woman whom my heart loved as a child. I would run behind her in the fields and cling to her skirts in the streets.

I knew her as a youth. I would see the image of her face in the pages of books and essays. I would see the outline of her body among the clouds in the sky and hear the melody of her voice rising with the rippling of streams.

I knew her when I was a man. I would sit with her talking and asking questions. I would come to her, complaining of the torments in my heart and telling her the secrets of my spirit.

All that was yesterday. Yesterday is a dream that will not return. But today this woman went to a distant land, barren, bleak, and cold, which they call the Land of Emptiness and Oblivion.

The name of the woman whom my heart loved is Life.

Life is a woman, a beautiful sorceress seducing our hearts, beguiling our spirits, flooding our being with promises. If she is put off, she kills patience within us. If she is faithful, she awakens boredom within us.

Life is a woman bathed in the tears of her lovers and perfumed with the blood of those she kills.

Life is a woman wearing the white robe of day lined with the black of night.

Life is a woman who with pleasure takes the human heart as a lover but rejects it as a husband.

Life is a harlot, but she is beautiful. Whoever sees her harlotry abhors her beauty.

A Smile and a Tear

*T*he sun gathered up her skirts and hurried away, leaving the green gardens to the subtle light pouring from the moon as it rose from behind the horizon. I sat there under the trees, thinking about how the air constantly changes from one state to another, and looking through the branches at stars scattered like silver coins on a dark blue carpet. Far away I heard the rippling of brooks in the valley.

When the birds had found shelter in their leafy nests, when the flowers had shut their eyes and silence ruled, I heard soft footsteps on the grass. I turned and saw a boy and a girl very close to me. They sat down beneath a lush tree. I could see them without being seen.

As soon as the youth had looked around, I heard him say, "Sit beside me, Beloved, and listen to me. Smile, for your smile is the symbol of our future. Rejoice, for the days have been happy because of you. My soul tells me of the doubt that pervades your heart. Doubt in love is sin, Beloved! Soon will you be mistress of all these broad estates, these lands lit by the silver moon. You will be lady of this palace, a palace rivaling the palaces of kings. My noble horses will draw you through parks, and handsome coaches will carry you to balls and amusements. Smile, Beloved, as the gold smiles in my treasuries. Gaze at me as you would gaze at my father's jewels. Hear me, Beloved. My heart insists on pouring out its secrets to you. Before us is a year of honeymoon. We will spend the year and much gold upon the shores of Switzerland's lakes, in the gardens of Italy, in palaces beside the Nile, and beneath the branches of the Cedars of Lebanon. You will meet princesses and ladies, and they will envy your jewels and clothes. All that you will have from me. Are you not content? Ah! How sweet is your smile. It foreshadows the smile of my fate."

After a little while I saw them walking slowly, crushing flowers beneath their feet as the rich man's foot crushes the poor man's heart.

When they were gone, I thought about the role of wealth in love. I thought about how wealth is the source of man's evils and of how love is the source of happiness and light.

I remained lost in these thoughts until I saw two shapes pass before of me. They sat down on the grass—

a boy and girl coming from the fields where the farm-
ers have their huts amid their crops. After a long
moment of touching silence, I heard these words. They
were mixed with the hoarse coughs of the consump-
tive. "Hold back your tears, Beloved. Love willed to
open our eyes and make us its servants so as to give us
the blessings of patience and endurance. Hold back
your tears and be consoled, for we are bound together
in the religion of love. Because of sweet love we can
bear the affliction of poverty, the bitterness of misery,
the torments of separation. I have no choice but to
struggle each day until I win a treasure worthy to lay
in your hands, a treasure to aid us in traveling on the
journeys of life. Love is God, Beloved. It accepts from
us our sighs and these tears as though they were the
smoke of incense, and it will recompense us as we
deserve. I bid you farewell, Beloved, for I must go be-
fore the moon sets."

Then I heard a soft voice, burning sobs, the voice
of a delicate maiden bidding farewell to all the heat of
love that was in her limbs and greeting the bitterness
of separation and the sweetness of endurance.
"Goodbye, Beloved."

They parted. I sat under the branches of that tree
feeling the hands of pity and the mysteries of this
strange existence pull at my being.

At that hour I looked toward sleeping nature and
thought a long time. I found something unbounded

and infinite there, something that could not be bought with money. I found something that could not be effaced by the tears of autumn nor killed by the sorrow of winter. It was something that you cannot find by the lakes of Switzerland nor in the gardens of Italy. I found something that endures, that gives life in spring, that gives fruit in summer. I found love there.

A Dialogue of Spirits

*A*wake, my beloved, awake! For my spirit calls to you from beyond fearful seas. My soul stretches its wings toward you over angry, foaming waves. Awake, for movement has ceased and silence has stilled the clamor of hoofbeats. The footsteps of passersby have ceased, and sleep has embraced the spirits of men. I alone remain awake, for longing pulls me to safety whenever slumber would drown me. Love draws me nigh to you whenever apprehension would pull me away. I leave my bed, beloved, fearful of dreams of oblivion concealed within the blankets' folds. I throw down my book, for my sighs have burned the lines from its pages and left them empty and white before my eyes. Awake, awake, my beloved, and hear me!

— *Thou, my love! I heard your call from beyond the seas and felt your wings brush me. I awoke and left my chamber and went into the fields. My feet and the hems of my robe*

wet with night dew, I stood beneath the flowering almond tree and listened to the call of your soul, my love.

—Speak, my beloved, and let your breaths flow with the wind blowing back to me from the valleys of Lebanon. Speak! Only I shall hear, for darkness has driven all creatures to their nests. All the people of the city are drunk with sleep, and only I remain to listen.

—*My love, the sky has woven a veil from moonlight and thrown it over the body of Lebanon.*

—My beloved, in the darkness of night the sky is a thick cloak, trapping the smoke of factories and the breaths of death, concealing the ribs of the city.

—*The villagers lie in the huts they have built among the walnut and willow trees, my love, and their souls race toward the theatres of dreams!*

—Heavy loads of gold have bent men's backs. Their caravans are weary from climbing the rocky paths of desire. Cares have made their eyelids heavy. They have thrown themselves upon their beds, my beloved, their hearts tormented by the phantoms of fear and despair.

—*The ghosts of past ages walk by night in the valleys. The spirits of kings and prophets hover about the mountain peaks. My thought turns toward the theatre of memory and shows me the glories of the Chaldeans, the splendor of Assyria, the greatness of the Arabs.*

—The dark spirits of thieves stalk the alleys by night and passions as adders' heads appear in the slits of windows. Through the twisting streets blow the breaths of the sick mingled with men's dying gasps. Memory pulls away the curtains of forgetfulness, showing me the vices of Sodom and the depravities of Gomorah.

—*The branches sway, my love, rustling with the purl of the valley brook. They echo in my ears like the Song of Solomon, the psalms of David's lyre, the melodies of Mawsili.*

—The souls of the neighbor children tremble, uneasy in their hunger. Sighs hasten from sleeping mothers, their brows furrowed with care and despair. Nightmares of poverty trouble the hearts of crippled men, and I hear bitter weeping and disjointed cries filling breasts with grief and regret.

—*The scent of narcissus and lily fill the air, and the perfumes of jasmine and elder mingle with the fresh breaths of the cedars. The breeze carries them by night above the hill-*

tops and twisted mountain paths to fill the soul with long-
ing and to make it yearn to glide in the air.

—Stench rises from foul alleys, from the ferment of
disease germs. Like sharp unseen arrows it rends the
senses and poisons the air.

—*The morning has come, my love. The fingers of wakeful-
ness have touched sleeping eyes. Violet rays stream from
beyond the night, rending the veil that had concealed the
energy and glory of life, arousing villages that had lain in
calm and silence on the slopes of the valley. Church bells
ring and fill the æther with their call, piously proclaiming
the start of morning worship, and the caves echo to their
voices as though all nature stood in prayer. Calves leave
their stalls. Flocks of sheep and goats leave their pens for
the fields, lowering their heads to crop the tips of grass glit-
tering with dew. Before them walk shepherds blowing their
flutes, behind them girls, greeting the morning with the spar-
rows.*

—The morning has come, my beloved, spreading heavy
hands of day above the crowded houses. Curtains are
drawn from the windows, and doors are pulled open
to reveal grey faces and worried eyes. The wretched
trudge to the factories, death dwelling within their
bodies beside life, their pinched features showing the

shadow of despair and fear, the shadow that would
darken the face of one sent against his will to a fearful
and deadly battle. The streets are choked with people
in greedy haste. The air is filled with the shock of steel,
the grinding of gears, the shriek of steam. The town
has become a battlefield where strong fight weak and
the tyrannous rich monopolize the fruits of the toil of
the poor and destitute.

—*How beautiful is life here, my love, for it is like the heart
of the poet, filled with life and delicacy!*

—How harsh is life here, my beloved, for it is like the
heart of a criminal, filled with vice and horrors!

THE BRIDAL BED[†]

*T*he bride and groom left the church with the happy guests following behind and torchbearers going before. Around them young men danced and girls sang songs of joy.

The procession reached the groom's house, now adorned with expensive furniture, glittering dishes, and fragrant herbs. The couple climbed onto a raised couch, and the guests sat down on silk carpets and velvet chairs, packing the large room. The servants hurried about with wine, and the clink of cups mixed with the happy shouts. Next musicians came and took their places, intoxicating the people with their magical voices and filling hearts with melodies woven on the hum-

---

[†] This incident took place in the north of Lebanon during the second half of the nineteenth century. I was told the story by a trustworthy woman related to one of the people in the story.

ming strings of the lute from men's sighs and the rus-
tling of the tambourine.

Then the girls stood up to dance, their bodies
swaying with the music as slender branches sway with
the breaths of the breeze. The folds of their soft dresses
moved like white clouds touched by moonlight. All
eyes were upon them and all heads bent to watch. The
spirits of the young men embraced them, and their
beauty broke old men's hearts. Then everyone turned
back to ask for more to drink, and their desires were
drowned in wine. They grew restless and their voices
grew louder. License ruled and dignity disappeared.
Brains were addled, souls burned, hearts were restless.
The whole house and everything in it became like a
guitar, its strings broken and plucked roughly by a
demoness, her song wavering between harmony and
discord. Here a young man reveals the secrets of his
love for a girl, coquettish and proud in her beauty.
Over there a youth arranges sweet words and subtle
hints in his mind as he prepares to talk to a beautiful
girl. A middle-aged man downs cup after cup and re-
peatedly asks the musicians to play songs that remind
him of his youth. In this corner a woman makes eyes
at a man, but he looks with love at another. In that
corner a woman, her hair white with age, smiles at the
girls trying to choose a bride for her only son. Stand-
ing by that window a wife whose husband is drunk
finds a chance to be with her lover. All are drowned in

a sea of wine and flirtation, have surrendered to a flood of exultation and pleasure, have forgotten the events of yesterday, have turned away from the morrow, have devoted themselves to exploiting the present moments.

The beautiful bride stared with unhappy eyes at the scene, a despairing prisoner gazing at her prison's black walls. Every few moments she would look to one corners of the room. A youth of twenty sat there, alone among the happy people, a wounded bird separate from its flock, his arms folded on his chest as though they kept his heart from flight. He stared at something invisible in the air of the room, as though his essence had departed from his visible body to soar in space with the phantoms of the night.

Midnight came. The noise of the crowd became frenzy. The guests' minds clouded with wine and their speech grew slurred. The bridegroom rose from his place. He was a middle-aged man, rough in appearance. Intoxication had dulled his senses. He walked among the guests, exchanging greetings and accepting congratulations.

At that moment the bride beckoned a girl to come and sit beside her. The bride looked around her like one who wished to confess a ghastly secret. She leaned toward the girl and whispered these words in her ear in a shaking voice, "I entreat you, my friend, by the affections that have bound our souls since we were children. I entreat you by all that is dear to you in this life, by the secrets of your heart, by the love that has touched our spirits and made them bright! I entreat you by the joys of your heart and by the torments of mine. Go this moment to Saleem and ask him to come secretly out to the garden and to wait for me there among the willows. Plead with him for me, Sosan, until he agrees. Remind him of days past. Beg him in the name of Love. Tell him, 'She is wretched and blind.' Tell him, 'She is dying and wants to open her heart to you before the shadows enshroud her.' Say to him, 'She is perishing with misery and wants only to see the light of your eyes before the fires of Hell snatch her away.' Tell him, 'She is a sinner who seeks to confess her sins and beg your forgiveness.' Hurry to him and plead with him for me! You need not fear that these swine will overhear you, for wine has blocked their ears and blinded their eyes."

Sosan rose from beside the bride and went to speak with the wretched Saleem, still sitting alone. She began to implore him, whispering into his ear the words of her friend, the proofs of affection and sincerity plain to see in her features. He turned his head to listen but gave no word in reply. When she finished talking, he looked at her as a thirsty man might look at a cup of water high above him in the dome of the sky. In a low voice that might have come up from the depths of the earth, he answered her, "I will wait for her in the garden among the willows."

He said these words and stood up to go into the garden.

Only a few minutes passed before the bride rose and followed him, looking furtively around herself at the men enamored with wine and at the women preoccupied with the remaining young men. She went out to the garden, concealed by the robes of night, hurrying like a terrified gazelle fleeing toward a thicket to escape hungry wolves. She reached the willow trees, and the young man was waiting. When she found herself beside him, she threw herself upon him, clung to his neck with her arms, and stared into his eyes. Then she spoke some hurried words, words pouring from her lips like the tears rushing from her eyes. "Listen, my love! Listen well. I have repented my ignorance and my haste. I have repented, Saleem, until repentance has crushed my heart. I love you, and I love no one else. I shall love you until the end of my life. They told me that you had forgotten me, that you had gone away from me, that you had fallen in love with another. They told me all that, Saleem, and their tongues poisoned my heart. Their nails tore my heart, and they filled my soul with lies. Najeeba told me that you had forgotten me, that you detested me, that you had fallen passionately in love with her. That evil woman wronged me and deceived my emotions so that I would be willing to take her kinsman as a husband. I agreed, Saleem, but I have no husband but you!

"Now, now the veil has been removed from my eyes, and I have come to you. I have left this house and I will not return to it. I have come to take you in my arms. There is no power in this world that could return me to the arms of the man whom in hatred and despair I accepted in marriage. I have abandoned the husband whom untruth chose to be my master. I have abandoned the father whom fate made my guardian. I have abandoned the flowers that the priest wove as my garland. I have abandoned the laws that custom has twisted into bonds. I have abandoned everything in this house, this house full of drunkenness and depravity. I have come to follow you to a distant land, to the ends of the earth, to the hidden houses of the jinn, into the hands of death.

"Come, we must hurry, Saleem, and leave this place under cover of night. We must go down to the coast and board a ship that will take us to distant unknown lands. Let us go now, so that when dawn comes we will be safe from the hands of our enemies. Look, look at this golden jewelry, these expensive necklaces and rings, these precious gems. They will provide for our future. The price will be sufficient for us to live like princes! Why do you say nothing, Saleem? Why don't you look at me? Why do you not kiss me? Do you not hear the cry of my heart and the screaming of my soul? Do you not believe that I have left my bridegroom, my father, my mother, and come in a wedding gown to flee with you? Say something, or let us hurry, for these moments are more precious than diamonds, more expensive than the crowns of kings."

As the bride spoke, her voice was a song sweeter than the whisper of life, more bitter than the cry of death, softer than the rustle of wings, deeper than the thunder of the surf—a song that vibrated with the alternation of despair and hope, of pleasure and pain, of joy and misery, of all the yearnings and emotions that are in the heart of a woman.

As the youth listened, love and honor struggled within his soul—the love that would make the rough path smooth and turn darkness into light, and the honor that stands before the soul and diverts it from its desires and passions. That love is sent down by God upon the heart. That honor is poured by human conventions into the brain.

Silent, terrifying moments passed, moments like dark centuries in which nations rise and fall. The youth raised his head. The nobility of his soul had gained control over its desire. He turned his eyes away from the frightened waiting girl and slowly said, "Woman, go back to the arms of your husband. The matter is settled, and awaking has erased the pictures painted by dreams. Go back to your wedding feast before watchful eyes see you and people start to say, 'She betrayed her husband on her wedding night just as she betrayed her lover while he was far away.'"

At these words, the bride began to tremble, shaking like a flower withering before the wind. In agony she said, "I will not return to this house, not even in the last breath of my life. I have left it forever. I have abandoned it and everyone in it just as the prisoner abandons the land of his exile. Do not send me away from you, and do not say that I am unfaithful, for the hand of love that bound my spirit to yours is stronger than the hand of the priest that delivered my body to the will of my husband. See, I have put my arms around your neck, and no force will release them. My soul has drawn near your soul, and not even death will separate them."

The youth tried to escape from her arms. In a voice of loathing and aversion, he said, "Leave me, woman. I have forgotten you. Yes, I have forgotten you and I detest you. My love now belongs to another. The people said no more than the truth. Have you heard what I said? I have forgotten you and no longer remember your existence. My hate for you is such that my soul recoils from your sight. Leave me, and let me go on my way. Go back to your husband and be a faithful wife to him!"

The tormented girl replied, "No! I do not believe what you say! You love me. I read words of love in your eyes, and I felt its touch when I touched your body. You love me. You love me as I love you. I will not leave this place except at your side. I will not go into this house so long as there is a remnant of free will within me. I came to follow you to the ends of the earth, so now you must seize me and spill my blood."

Raising his voice, the young man said, "Leave me, woman, or I will shout and call into the garden all these people who have been invited to share the joys of your wedding. I will show them your shame and make you a bitter morsel in their mouths, an object of scorn on their tongues. At my bidding Najeeba, whom my heart loves, will mock you, laughing in her victory and scorning you in your defeat."

As he said this, as he took her arms to push her from him, her features changed. Her eyes blazed. All her entreaty, hope, and pain turned to anger and cruelty. She became a lioness who has lost her cubs, a sea, its depths stirred by hurricanes. "Who will enjoy your love after me? Which heart other than mine will be drunk with the kisses of your lips?"

When she had spoken these words, she drew a sharp dagger out of her gown and like lightning thrust it into his breast. He fell to the ground, a branch torn by the storm. She bent over him, the dripping dagger still in her hand. He opened eyes blurred by the shadow of death and from his trembling lips these words came with his weak breaths, "Come to me now, Beloved. Come to me, Layla, and do not leave me. Life is weaker than death, but death is weaker than love. Listen, do you hear the laughter of the guests at your

wedding? Do you hear the clattering of their cups, Beloved? You have delivered me, Layla, from the torment of that laughter and the bitterness of that wine. Let me kiss the hand that broke my chains. Kiss my lips, kiss these lips that tried to lie and that concealed the secrets of my heart. Close my dimming eyes with fingers stained with my blood. When my spirit takes flight into space, put the dagger into my right hand and say to them that I killed myself in despair and jealousy. I love you, Layla, and I love no other, but I imagined that it would be better to sacrifice my heart, my happiness, and my life than to run away with you on your wedding night. Kiss me, beloved of my soul, before people see my body. Kiss me, kiss me, Layla!"

The fallen man placed his hand above his wounded heart, turned his head, and gave up his spirit.

The bride raised her head and, turning toward the house, cried in an awful voice, "Come, come, O people! The wedding is here, and this is the bridegroom. Come, so that we can show you our soft bridal bed. Awake, sleepers! Drunkards, come to your senses, and come quickly. We will show you the mysteries of love and death and life!"

The bride's cry echoed in the corners of the house, carrying her words to the ears of the happy celebrants. Their spirits shuddered, and they listened for a moment as though sobriety had surprised them in their intoxication. Then they poured out of the house, looking to right and left as they went. When they saw the body of the fallen man and the bride kneeling near him, they drew back in horror. No one dared ask what had happened, for the blood flowing from the breast of the murdered man and the glint of the dagger in the hand of the bride had tied their tongues and frozen their spirits within them.

The bride turned toward them. A sad dignity clothed her features. "Draw near, cowards," she shouted. "You need not fear the ghost of death, for it is great and will not come near your pettiness. Come close. You do not have to tremble in fear of this dagger. It is a sanctified instrument that will not touch your filthy bodies and dark breasts. Look at this handsome young man, dressed for the wedding. He is my lover. I killed him because he is my lover. He is my husband, and I am his bride. We searched but could find no bridal bed worthy of our embrace in this world, which you have made so narrow by your customs, so dark by your ignorance, so corrupt by your lust. We have preferred to go somewhere beyond the clouds. Come near and look, you weak and frightened people. Perhaps you will see the face of God reflected on our faces and hear His sweet voice pouring out of our hearts. Where is she, that wicked and jealous woman, who slandered my lover to me? She said that he had conceived a passion for her and had forgotten me, that he had given his love to her in order to forget me. That wicked woman imagined that she had triumphed when the priest raised his hand above my head and the head of her kinsman. Where is the deceitful Najeeba? Where is that hellish viper? Let her come and see that she has gathered you to celebrate the wedding of my lover, not the wedding of the man she chose for me.

"You do not understand what I say, for the depths of the sea cannot contain the planets' songs, but you will tell your children of the woman who killed her lover on her wedding night. You will remember me, and you will curse me with your sinful lips, but your descendents will bless me, for tomorrow will belong to truth and the spirit.

"And you, the foolish man who used deceit, wealth, and malice to make me his wife—you are the symbol of this wretched nation that seeks light in darkness, that sits waiting for water to gush from the rock and for roses to appear on the thorn bush. You are the symbol of this country, which in blind folly has surrendered to a blind leader. You are the representative of the false manhood that cuts off a head or a hand to steal a necklace or a bracelet. I forgive you your pettiness, for the soul rejoicing in departing this world forgives all the sins of this world."

Then the bride raised the dagger above her like a thirsty man raising a cup's brim to his lips. She sheathed the dagger firmly in her breast and fell beside her lover, a lily cut down by the scythe. The women flinched and cried out in fear and pain. A few fainted. The clamor of the men arose on every side, and they approached the fallen pair with dread and awe.

The dying bride stared at them, bright blood pouring from her crystal breast. "Don't come near, you who would censure me, and do not separate our bodies. Should you do so, the spirit that circles over your heads will seize your throats and strangle you cruelly. Let this hungry earth consume our bodies in a single bite. Let it conceal us and protect us in its breast as it protects the seeds from the snows of winter until the coming of spring."

The bride gripped her lover and kissed his cold lips. Her last disjointed words came with her last breaths: "Look, Beloved! Look, husband of my soul, how the envious stand about our bed! See how they stare at us! Hear the grinding of their teeth and the snapping of their ribs! You have waited a long time for me, Saleem. Now, see how the shackles have broken and the chains snap. Let us hurry toward the Sun, for we have waited too long in the shadow. Forms are erased and beings are veiled, and I no longer see anything but you, Beloved. Here are my lips. Receive my last breaths. Let us go, Saleem! Love has spread its wings and flies before us to the circle of light."

The bride threw herself upon her lover's breast, and her blood mingled with his. She rested her head upon his neck, and her eyes stared fixed into his eyes.

The people remained silent for a moment, their faces pale and their knees weak, as though the dread of death had stolen their power to move.

Then the priest came forward, he whose teachings had woven the garland of that wedding. With his right hand he pointed at the slain pair. To the bewildered people, he said, "Cursed will be the hands that reach out to these two bodies, stained with the blood of crime and shame! Cursed the eyes that shed tears of sorrow, for devils bear their damned souls down to Hell! The corpses of this son of Sodom and this daughter of Gomorrah shall lie upon the impure earth, this dust kneaded with their blood, until dogs consume their flesh and the winds scatter their bones. People, go to your homes and flee the stench that rises from within two hearts conceived in sin and destroyed by vice. Go, ye who stand near these two corpses, and hurry away before you are stung by the tongues of hellfire! Whoever among you remains will be excommunicated and will be forbidden to enter a church where the believers kneel in prayer and to partake of the mass offered by Christians!"

Sosan, the girl whom the bride had sent as a messenger to her lover, came and stood by the priest. She looked at him with eyes drowning in tears. Bravely she said, "I will remain here, O blinded unbeliever. I will guard them until the dawn comes. I will dig them a grave beneath these hanging branches. If you will not

give me a spade, I will scratch the earth with my fin-
gers, and if you bind my arms, I will dig it with my
teeth! Hurry and leave this place, this place filled with
the scent of frankincense, for swine avoid the scent of
pure perfumes and the thief dreads the owner of the
house and the coming of the morn. Hurry to your dark
beds. The angels' songs that fill the air above these two
martyrs to love do not reach you, for your ears are
plugged with dirt."

The people dispersed before the grim face of the
priest. That girl remained, standing near the two still
bodies like a watchful mother guarding her children in
the stillness of the night.

When the crowd had gone and that place was
empty, she gave herself over to weeping and grief.

In the Name of God, My Heart

*I*n the Name of God, my heart,
conceal your passion.
Better to hide your complaint from those
who see you.

He who reveals secrets
is like the foolish man.
Silence and concealment
is better for him who loves.

In the Name of God, my heart, if someone
comes to ask, hide what befell me.

If they say, my heart,
"Who does he desire?"
Say, "She seduced another.
He does not care."

In the Name of God, my heart, veil your ardor.
You know this disease has made you weak.

Love among spirits
is like wine in a cup.
It appears to be water,
but in truth is life.

In the Name of God, my heart, lock up your cares.
You will be safe though seas rage and heavens fall.

WHAT IS HIDDEN
IN HEARTS

A stately house stood in the darkness of the night, like life among the curtains of death. A beautiful girl sat at an ivory writing table, her head resting on her hand like a wilted iris blossom leaning on its leaves. She stared around her, as a prisoner who has lost all hope that his eyes might pierce the walls of his jail to see life going by in free procession.

Hours passed with the phantoms of the night as that girl sought companionship in her tears, sought safety in her loneliness and lovesickness, as her emotions trampled her heart and her feelings seized the keys of the treasuries where her heart's secrets were hid. She took up a pen. At first tears blotted the lines of ink on the paper, uniting words and the secrets of her soul. This is what she wrote:

"Beloved sister,

"When secrets straiten the heart, when eyes are made raw by hot tears, and ribs nearly crack from the swelling of what is hidden in the breast, man can find no comfort but in words and complaint. Sorrow, my friend, is eased by complaint. The lover finds solace in words of longing. The oppressed finds pleasure in seeking mercy. . . So I write to you. I have become like the poet who sees beauty and who records, compelled by the power of his divine nature, the impressions of that beauty in verse. I am like the poor and hungry child who, driven by the bite of his hunger, pleads with his mother for succor, unmindful of her poverty and destitution.

"My sister, listen to my story of pain and weep for me, for weeping is like prayer and tears of sympathy are like the good deed that is always requited, for they come up from the depths of a living and sensitive soul.

"As he had wished, my father gave me in marriage to a rich and important man. Like other fathers of wealth and station, he feared that one day poverty and degradation would come. Thus, he sought to join wealth to wealth and station to high station.

"Despite my own desires and dreams I was sacrificed on an altar of the gold and the inherited honor that I despise. I was held trembling in the talons of matter, that beast of prey—for when matter is not tamed and made obedient to the spirit, it is crueler than death and more bitter than the pit of Hell. I respect my husband, for he is kind and noble-hearted and seeks my happiness. He spends his wealth freely to please me, but none of this is equal to a moment of true and sanctified love, love that makes all else seem petty while remaining itself great.

"Do not laugh at me, my friend, for no one knows the needs of a woman's heart better than I—this beating heart, this bird soaring in the air of love, this goblet brimming with wine pressed through the ages as a drink for spirits, this book in which are printed chapters of happiness and grief, of pleasure and pain, of joys and sorrows, and which will be read only by him who was created as her other half before eternity and for all eternity. . . Yes, I have come to know women. I knew the desires of their souls, the longings of their hearts, at that moment when I found that my husband's proud horses, his splendid carriages, his overflowing coffers and high station were not worth a single glance from the eyes of that poor youth who came into this life for my sake, and I for his. That youth is patient in the anguish of tribulation and the misery of separation, oppressed by being destroyed by my father's decision, imprisoned for no crime in the darkness of life. Beware, my friend, of trying to comfort me, for I have a comforter in my afflictions. It is my apprehension of the power of my love, my knowledge of the nobility of my desire and yearning. Now I look from behind my tears and see my fate drawing nearer day by day. It will lead me to the place where my soul's companion awaits me. There I will meet him and take him in a long and holy embrace. You have no reason to criticize me. I do what a faithful wife must. Patient and calm I am obedient to human laws. I honor my husband in my mind and respect him with my heart, give him honor with my soul. But I cannot give him my whole being. God gave it to my lover before ever I knew my lover. For some hidden wisdom Heaven willed that I spend my life with a man though I was created for another. I will spend this life in silence, as Heaven wills. When the gates of eternity open, I will be joined to my fair half and I will look to the past—that past which is this moment—as the spring looks back at the winter. I will contemplate this life of mine as one who has reached the summit of a mountain contemplates the steep paths he has climbed."

The girl now ceased writing and covered her face with her hand, weeping bitterly, as though her great soul bridled at putting her most sacred thoughts on paper but instead revealed them as hot tears soon dried, mingling with the subtle æther, the homeland of lovers' breaths and the scent of blossoms. After a moment she took the pen and began to write: "My friend, do you remember that youth? Do you remember the light shining from his eyes and the sorrows engraved in his brow? Do you remember his smile, a smile like the

tears of a mother who has lost her child? Do you re-
member his voice, like an echo in a distant valley? Do
you remember his long thoughtful looks as he consid-
ered something, how he would then speak of it in an
unusual way? How he would then bow his head and
sigh as though he feared that his words would reveal
the secrets of his great heart? Do you remember his
dreams and his beliefs? Do you remember how all these
things were in a youth whom men reckoned to be only
a man and whom my father belittled because he was
above earthly desires and too noble to inherit nobility
from his ancestors? My sister, you know that I am a
martyr to the petty things of this world, a sacrifice to
its stupidity. You will pity a sister who watches wake-
ful in the silence of the fearful night revealing the secrets
of her heart to you. You will pity her, for love has also
visited your heart."

When the morning came, the girl at last fell asleep,
perhaps to find there dreams finer than the dreams of
wakefulness.

Daughters of the Sea

*I*n the depths of the sea surrounding the islands far to the east, in the depths where many pearls are found, floated the dead body of a young man. The golden-haired daughters of the sea gathered around it. They sat on ridges of coral looking at it with bright blue eyes. The deep sea heard their musical voices. The waves bore their voices to the shores, and the breeze carried them to my soul.

One said, "This man died yesterday when the sea was angry."

A second said, "The sea was not angry, but rather Man, he who claims to be descended from the gods. Much blood was spilled in a fierce war, and the sea turned scarlet. This man was killed in the war."

A third said, "I do not know what war is, but I know that after Man conquered the dry land, he lusted to rule the sea. He devised strange machines and ploughed the sea. Neptune, god of the seas, learned of this and grew angry at this transgression. Man could only seek to placate our lord with sacrifices and gifts. The corpses that fell yesterday were but the latest offering from Man to great Neptune."

A fourth said, "How great is Neptune, but how cruel is his heart! Were I the queen of the seas, I would not be pleased with bloody sacrifices. Come, I will show you the corpse of this youth. Perhaps we will learn something of the tribe of man."

The daughters of the sea surrounded the body of the youth and began to search his clothes. They found a letter in a pocket next to his heart and read:

"My love, it is midnight. I sit wakeful with no one to comfort me save my tears, nothing to console me save my hope that you will return to me from among the talons of war. I can think of nothing save what you said to me when we parted, that each person is entrusted with a tear, which he must someday return. I do not know, my love, what it is that I write. I give my soul leave to flow onto the paper—a soul is tormented by misery and consoled by love that transforms pain into pleasure and sorrows into joy. . . When love united our hearts and we awaited the union of our two bodies in a single spirit, the war called you and you obeyed, compelled by necessity and patriotism. But what is this necessity that separates lovers and makes women into widows and children orphans? What is this patriotism that turns small causes into a war that will destroy countries? What is this necessity that binds the poor villager but does not trouble the powerful or the aristocrat? If necessity destroys peace among nations and patriotism troubles the quiet of human life, then farewell to necessity and patriotism! No, no, my love! Pay no attention to my words. Rather be brave and love your country. Do not listen to the words of a girl blinded by love, whose vision is clouded by separation. If love does not return you to me in this life, then love will unite me with you in the life to come."

The daughters of the sea replaced that letter in the youth's pocket and swam away in silent sorrow. When they were far away, one of them said, "Truly man's heart is crueler than the heart of Neptune!"

O NIGHT

*N*ight of lovers, poets, musicians!
Night of phantoms, spirits, ghosts!
Night of passionate longing and remembrance!
Giant standing among the petty clouds in the West,
among the brides of the morn, girded with a fearful
sword, rolling with the moon, robed in silence, staring
with a thousand eyes into the depths of life, listening
with a thousand ears to the last breath of death and
non-being!

You are the darkness that shows us starlight,
though the brightness of the day veils us in the dark-
ness of earth.

You are the hope that opens our eyes before
infinity's awe, but the day is a delusion that makes us
as blind men in the world of finite quantities.

You are a peace whose stillness unfolds the mysteries of those awakened spirits who soar in the highest heaven. Day is a noise whose effects trouble the souls of those trampled under the hooves of desires and novelties.

In deep darkness you are the just ruler who reconciles the dreams of the weak and the hopes of the strong. You are tender, you whose invisible fingers gently close the eyes of the wretched, bearing their hearts to a world less harsh than this.

Lovers whisper among the folds of your blue-black robe. The desolate spill their tears at your dew-covered feet. Exiles place their sighs of helpless yearning in your palms, your palms perfumed with the scents of the valleys. Thus are you the confidant of lovers, the friend of the lonely, the companion of the exile and the desolate.

The sentiments of poets steal through your shadows. The hearts of the prophets are borne upon your shoulders. Among your tresses is found the genius of thinkers. You instruct the poets, inspire the prophets, advise the people of thought and contemplation.

When my soul wearies of people and my eyes tire of staring into the face of day, I go to those distant fields where the ghosts of past ages become still.

There I stand before a dark and solid being, a being that trembles and goes upon a thousand feet above the plains and mountains and valleys.

There I stand staring with eyes of darkness, listening to the rustle of unseen wings, sensing the touch of robes of silence, courageous among the terrors of the dark.

There I see you, Night, a fearful beautiful form rising between earth and heaven, clothed in clouds, wrapped in mist, laughing at the sun and mocking the day, scorning the creatures sitting wakeful before their idols, raging at kings sleeping beneath silk and brocade, staring at the faces of thieves, watching near the cradles of infants, weeping at the smiles of the depraved, smiling at the tears of lovers, raising with your right hand great hearts, crushing beneath your feet petty souls.

There I see you, Night, and you see me. You are a father to me, though I fear you, and in my dreams I am your son. The veils of obscurity are removed from between us and the veils of doubt and conjecture are torn from our faces. You reveal to me your secret intentions, and I tell you plainly my hopes and desires. At last your terrors are transformed into a song sweeter than the whispers of flowers. My fears become a friendship more dear than the peace of the thrush. You bear me up to you and seat me upon your shoulders. You teach my eyes to see and my ears to hear and my lips to speak. You teach my heart to love that which men do not love and to hate that which men do not hate. Then you touch my thoughts with your fingertips, and my thoughts pour out like a river rushing and singing as it washes away the withered grass. Then you kiss my spirit with your lips, and my spirit reels like a spark that sets aflame idols of dry wood.

I was your companion, Night, until I became like you. I was your friend until my desires mixed with yours. I loved you until my being was transformed into a microcosm of your being. In my darkened soul stars shone, stars strewn in the evening by ecstasy, but the apprehensions of morning swept them away. Sometimes in my watchful heart a moon hurries across a sky, a sky sometimes obscured by clouds and sometimes crowded with the caravans of dreams. In my watchful spirit the shapes of silence reveal lovers' thoughts and its caves echo with the prayers of monks. There is a veil of magic wrapped about my head. The death-rattle of the dying tears at it, then the songs of the love-poets mend it again.

Night, I am like you. Will men think I am boasting when I liken myself to you? In their boasting they compare themselves to fire.

I am like you, for we are both accused of being what we are not.

I am like you in my desires and my dreams and my being and my character.

I am like you, though the evening does not crown me with golden clouds.

I am like you, though the morn does not stud my robes with the rosy light.

I am like you, though I am not girded with the Milky Way.

I am night—intimate, joyous, tranquil, troubled. My darkness has no beginning and my depths no end. When the spirits arise, splendid in the light of their joys, my spirit comes frozen in the shadows of its pain.

Night, I am like you. My morn will not come until my time has ended.